House Beautiful

STORAGE WORKSHOP

HouseBeautiful

STORAGE WORKSHOP

TESSA EVELEGH

HEARST BOOKS
A Division of Sterling Publishing Co., Inc.
New York

Created, edited, and designed by
Duncan Baird Publishers Ltd.,
Castle House, 75–76 Wells Street, London W1T 3QH

Managing Editor: Emma Callery
Designer: Alison Shackleton

Library of Congress Cataloging-in-Publication Data
Available
1 2 3 4 5 6 7 8 9 10

Published by Hearst Books
A Division of Sterling Publishing Co., Inc.
387 Park Avenue South, New York, NY 10016

House Beautiful is a registered trademark of Hearst
Communications, Inc.

www.housebeautiful.com

For information about custom editions, special sales,
premium and corporate purchases, please contact Sterling
Special Sales Department at 800-805-5489 or
specialsales@sterlingpub.com.

Distributed in Canada by Sterling Publishing
℅ Canadian Manda Group, 165 Dufferin Street
Toronto, Ontario, Canada M6K 3H6

Distributed in Australia by Capricorn Link (Australia)
Pty. Ltd.
P.O. Box 704, Windsor, NSW 2756 Australia

Manufactured in China
ISBN 13: 978-1-58816-589-3
ISBN 10: 1-58816-589-2

CONTENTS

FOREWORD

Whatever kind of house you have and whatever your style, it's a pretty safe bet that you would like more or better storage in your home. Chances are good that you need more storage because unless you're a storage expert (in which case, you probably wouldn't be looking at this book), it's very unlikely that your storage exactly suits your needs. Why is this?

First, because most people make do with the storage capabilities they inherited with the house, which may have never ideally suited anyone. At best, it will have suited the previous owners.

Second, if you haven't taken a good look at your family lifestyle in the last five years, you are likely unaware of the way the storage needs of your household have changed.

Third, because we're living in a consumption-oriented society, you're likely to have acquired more new possessions than you realize or would like to admit.

Fourth, because storage has come a long way in recent years, and there is an ever-increasing choice of furniture, systems, and interior fixtures and accessories.

The reason storage has progressed so much recently is that, especially in densely populated urban centers, living areas are generally becoming smaller and there is greater demand for efficient use of space and clever interior fixtures designed to meet those needs. With improved storage and efficient systems, your life can be so much better organized. All that picking up and putting away can be significantly streamlined, freeing you for much more enjoyable use of your time.

So where do you begin? The best place is with yourself, your things, and your lifestyle. These are the topics tackled in the first section of the book, aimed at helping you think about what would be right for you. It really is worth considering your own particular lifestyle in as much detail

as you can, rather than keeping with the most obvious, traditional solutions. For example, you may never have questioned the eye-level rod that is traditionally built into closets. But when you come to think of it, you don't own any full-length gowns and you might be better off with two clothing rods set one above the other. This is a theme that runs throughout the book. It is discussed in general in the first section and then revisited in greater detail later on when we look at storage room by room.

The second section of the book looks at different storage styles and which are best suited both to your interior design and lifestyle. Finally, the third section looks at each room with its particular storage needs with the aim of helping you work out what would be right for your lifestyle. The illustrated pages at the end of each room section look at some of the latest storage solutions and how they can be applied in various situations.

Storage plays a major role in any household, not just because it can so greatly affect the efficient running of the home, but because it also contributes to the overall look. With everything put away in its place, the interior style of your home can be so much better appreciated.

This is a book that we hope you will find useful for many years, revisiting it every time you want to sort out your interior space—whether to remodel the house completely or simply thinking about one corner of one room. Transcending style and fashion, it's aimed at helping you get control of your possessions, make maximum use of space, and ultimately streamline your chores for a much more organized, comfortable household.

From the Editors of *House Beautiful*

GETTING STARTED

EVERYTHING IN ITS PLACE

Effective storage solutions can have a greater positive impact on our lives than almost any other element in home design. Whether you love super-sleek modern minimalism, or Bohemian-style clutter, things run so much more smoothly when the storage is well thought out to suit your particular lifestyle and needs.

It's no coincidence that one of the abiding Shaker aphorisms is "a place for everything and everything in its place." They knew only too well that unless every member of their eighteenth-century community could lay his hands on what he needed when he needed it, the smooth running of their lives would be impeded. To this end, they designed efficient built-in wall-to-wall, floor-to-ceiling systems of drawers and cupboards, perfectly divided to accommodate all their daily needs. If everyone returned everything

▶ **All-in-one**
Here's a clever idea that offers efficient office space within a hallway.

▼ **Flush with success**
Modern flush cupboards stretching the full height and length of the wall provide surprising capacity without noticeably reducing the room dimensions.

to its designated storage place, they reasoned, then everyone else would be able to find it when needed. It's an excellent principle that works perfectly in theory.

However, in real life, it isn't always so simple. For a start, most of us are somewhat more acquisitive than the spartan Shakers, who never possessed anything beyond their basic needs. As a result, we never seem to have quite enough storage space and are often left pondering what to do with stuff that won't fit. Besides, few adult members of most families, let alone the children, are quite as disciplined at putting everything away as those well-organized Shakers. But even if we don't feel we measure up to the Shaker ideal, with careful consideration and clever design, we can work out the best storage solutions to suit both our belongings and the way we like to live. This will make the chores of both straightening up and finding what we need speedier and more efficient, giving us not only more time to do the things we'd really like to do, but helping us to feel better organized and in control of our lives.

▶ **Pretty and practical**
Exquisite antique chests with double bow fronts are lovely pieces of bedroom furniture and offer excellent storage for sweaters and shirts.

▶▶ **Super sleek**
Modern cabinets are often so sleek they're disguised as walls, fitted flush and devoid of handles. Opening the doors is easy, using a push mechanism. Here, a whole wall incorporates both cupboards and drawers, providing copious space for all your bedroom storage needs.

TAKE CONTROL: ASSESS YOURSELF

Are you a naturally organized person, never happier than when putting everything neatly in its place? Do you get satisfaction from perfectly stacked sweaters and color-coordinated closets? Or do you frankly find filing and straightening boring, a chore best done as speedily as possible? Do you prefer to conceal clutter behind closed doors, or do you love the decorative qualities of your favorite possessions?

These are questions you need to ask yourself before you even begin to plan the storage. They will help you decide how much you'd like to have on display; how many open shelves you may prefer; and what proportion of closets you'd like. Even once you've decided, consider the details. For example, are you a "piler" or a "hanger?" You might love the look of a pile of perfectly laundered and folded shirts, but if your hurried mornings mean you don't have the time or the patience to carefully

remove the one you need, your pile will soon be a jumbled mess! If that's a scenario you recognize, you might be happier hanging things up. Even T-shirts can be hung up one to a hanger and removed, when needed, without disturbing their closest neighbors.

In the home office, is the look of matching files on a shelf more important to you than a row of multi-colored files arranged in easy-to-find categories? These won't necessarily be yes or no answers, as both scenarios may be important to you—so you could choose files in a range of pleasing colors to stack on open shelves or hide inexpensive files in less than gorgeous colors behind cupboard doors. It is well worth going through every room of the house and asking yourself similar questions. There really are no right or wrong answers, but they will shed light on the solutions that are right for you.

▶ **All booked up**
People who love books tend to keep them on display, so divide the shelves vertically, both for strength and for visual interest.

▶▶ **Classic winner**
A pretty glass-front cupboard painted in a light color is a classic piece that works well in both modern and traditional interiors. Its contents can be used to make a decorative display, adding personality to the room.

TAKE CONTROL: ASSESS YOUR NEEDS

Storage needs are continually changing. Most obviously, needs change dramatically when a baby arrives, along with what seems like an inordinate amount of gear for one very small person. The toys at this stage can generally be contained within the crib and stroller, but as she heads for toddlerdom, they multiply alarmingly and distribute themselves throughout the house. They also change in scale, growing in size to a certain point, then generally becoming more and more diminutive, all of which demand different storage. For a child's room, you may, for example, choose a modular storage system that can be expanded or adapted annually as the child's needs change.

Then, as the family grows, you'll find that the kitchen may need more storage, while in the living room, whether or not you have children, you may find your media storage needs expanding. Books, too, are inclined to multiply, so you either need to allow for overflow book storage or be hard-nosed about weeding out volumes. The common factor in all these scenarios is planning for change. If you're thinking through storage needs having recently moved, try to imagine the future and assess what these are likely to be in five or even ten years' time.

The other aspect of assessing your needs is to consider the items that you would like to store and design appropriate storage to fit them. So, for example, instead of keeping one high hanging rod simply because it's there, count up how many full-length garments you have. You may be better off fitting two rods, one above the other, to accommodate more shirts and jackets, and then folding long garments into boxes, shelves, or drawers.

▶ **Divide and rule**
The shelves in this glass-front cabinet are divided to make for efficient book storage. You can store CDs and DVDs by stacking them into boxes that fit neatly on the shelves.

▶▶ **Hidden away**
A wall of closets runs down the left-hand side of this room, but you would barely know it. If you enjoy minimalist surroundings, such storage space is just what you need.

TAKE CONTROL: ASSESS YOUR HOME

Most of us inherit the storage arrangements that came with the house when we moved in. However, you may need to remodel some rooms, and this is your chance to rethink the storage completely to suit your needs. You might, for example, be able to install new closets along one bedroom wall, making use of what may currently be wasted space. Or you may be able to use the shell of the available closets, but redo their interiors to make better use of the space (see pages 110–111). Similarly, the kitchen may currently be fitted with cabinets that barely suit your needs. You might find that by equipping it with large drawers with appropriate dividers or a pantry module with sliding shelves, you could make much better use of vertical as well as horizontal space (see pages 82–83). Open shelves in any room can provide an effective solution that makes stylish, highly efficient, and very economical use of the space, especially if you can adjust them to fit the items you wish to store on them.

▶ **Period details**
The wooden bookcases in this period home have been given molding to blend with the architecture of their surroundings.

▼ **Making gains**
One can squeeze efficient storage from even the smallest spaces. Here, just 12 inches borrowed from the room means that roomy cupboards can be created all along one wall.

Since Colonial times, efficient built-in closets with doors paneled to match the rest of the walls were often incorporated into the original floor plan. Federal homes featured pretty display shelves that were sometimes set into walls. It is better to restore rather than replace these features, as they contribute to the character of the building, enhancing the overall design. In modern homes, too, storage is often built into the original framing, providing efficient use of space. If you're fitting storage systems into an existing building, it is generally best to be sensitive to the original architecture. So built-in bookshelves, for example, can be linked into the design of the room by matching the molding and trim. However, there are exceptions. In working rooms, such as kitchens, where function is all-important, it might be more appropriate to install sleek modern modules or island units. These can provide an elegant contrast to original architectural detail.

▲ In style
Reeded pilasters on either side of shelves built into an alcove perfectly complement the Federal-style fireplace, giving a cohesive look to the room.

▶ In the brickwork
Bookshelves incorporated into the curved walls of this elegant Modern home make excellent use of space, while enhancing the architecture.

SOMETHING FROM NOTHING

There's nothing new about built-in storage: the Shakers were masters at it, and it was often a feature of the best Colonial homes. These ideas have followed into the most modern homes with wall-to-wall closets, which make efficient use of space by stealing a little from the room's overall dimensions, but paying back dividends in terms of the volume of storage space. Using this principle, even if you're not in the fortunate position of building from scratch, there is a lot that can be done to incorporate large amounts of extra storage when remodeling your home.

As well as installing wall-to-wall closets in bedrooms or fitting modules in kitchens, analyze other potentially "dead" space in other parts of your home. A few inches chiseled from the side of a hallway, for example, can offer plenty of storage volume, especially when fitted with custom shelves (see also pages 132–133).

▶ **On the side**
A few inches have been taken from the width of this landing to make space for generous closets, which, when furnished with shelves, offer generous returns in terms of storage.

▶▶ **Three for two**
Two rooms have been opened up to provide a bedroom with an en suite bathroom. Closets borrow a little space from each of the original rooms to provide a generous dressing room.

SOMETHING FROM NOTHING: NICHES

Make use of any niches you might have by fitting them with shelves to create delightful displays of smaller possessions. Alternatively, if you need to store items that are more practical than beautiful, doors can be made to enclose the niches to create neat, flush cupboards. With narrow interior shelves, items can be stacked in a single row with everything visible, which makes an easy job of finding what you need.

You can make practical use of even the most diminutive and unpromising space by using it to store small items. For example, if your niche is in the kitchen, it can be used as a can or spice rack; in the bedroom, to keep lipsticks and nail polishes; in the bathroom, for toothbrushes. Niches can also be set into walls as an architectural detail, and then used for decorative display.

▲ **Neat feature**
This Federal-style plaster niche has been built into the wall to create a delightful architectural detail while providing storage for a collection of pitchers and tureens.

▲ **Open house**
For added interest, leave the door off a cupboard and display your favorite objects on the open shelves—a modern-day take on old-fashioned niches.

▲ Slim solution

This inches-deep niche makes excellent storage for serving pieces when wooden battens are added to keep them safely in place.

◀ Pretty clever

Trimmed with delicate lace edging, the shelves in this niche provide excellent storage for an array of blue-and-white dishes.

STORAGE STYLE

STORAGE FILE

Before you can begin to plan the storage, you need to work out what style would suit both you and your home. Do you love the look of traditional free-standing furniture that brings personality to the room, or are you more of a sleek, modern person whose priority is to keep the home neat, and quickly at that? The architecture of your home need not dictate which way you have to go, but the storage will need to be sensitive to the original design of the house. For example, if you have a beautiful home with exquisite period detail, you'd probably rather not cover that up. Instead, if you decide on wall-to-wall cabinets, you have two basic options. Either team them with the detail in the rest of the room by giving them matching baseboards and crown moldings, or use pared-back modern closets as a contrast to the existing period detailing. This will work if existing details, such as the original casings, are not damaged. By the same token, a beautiful painted armoire can look exquisite as a feature in

▶ **In keeping**

This storage unit has been given typical Adam styling that was popular during the Federal period. Although it is a fairly recent addition to the house, attention to detail has given it a permanent feel. Particularly note the reeded pilasters, molded garlands and urns, and the crown moldings at the top.

▶ **Design strength**

Shorter shelves have more strength than those with long spans, so aim to include vertical dividers. Here, double verticals have been aligned to the ceiling brackets to add a bit of visual interest.

an otherwise simple, modern interior. You don't have to be restricted to one style running throughout the house. What works in the bedroom, for example, may not be appropriate in the kitchen. Likewise, however much you may want to keep to traditional freestanding storage in most of the house, you may prefer to go modern in the kitchen, simply because that is easier to keep clean and tidy.

If you live in a Modern home, chances are you are making do with existing storage. However, if this doesn't meet your needs, you can always update it by refitting the interiors with all the latest space-saving devices (see the illustrated pages at the end of each room section). These can hugely improve the efficiency of your current storage.

The other consideration when planning the storage is to decide if you're the kind of family that loves to enjoy all their favorite possessions out in the open. Or perhaps you'd prefer everything safely stacked behind doors, both out of reach of youngsters and out of sight, leaving sleek, clear surfaces.

▼ **Understated elegance**
Kitchen modules were the first modern storage units to be accepted universally in the 1950s and '60s. These have evolved into sleeker, pared-down pieces, such as this bank, designed for streamlined practicality rather than homeyness.

◀ Double effect
Built-in closets and drawers installed along the full length of a short wall in a long, thin bedroom not only make efficient use of space, but reduce the length of the bedroom to create more pleasing overall proportions.

TRADITIONAL STORAGE

Much of traditional storage is freestanding: wardrobes, armoires, chests of drawers, sideboards, and dressers. They were designed and made by highly skilled cabinet-makers, such as Thomas Chippendale, who catalogued the styles of the time in his eighteenth-century classic, *Gentleman and Cabinet-Maker's Director*. His pieces, which adopted rococo, Gothic, and Chinoiserie styles, became the benchmark of fine furniture, and are still highly desirable reproduction pieces. The furnished feel that traditional storage furniture lends to a room has ensured its enduring popularity. Although Chippendale generally favored the polished wood look, the traditional style of painted Swedish furniture has always offered an elegant alternative and has enjoyed a renaissance in recent decades, mixing well with the lighter finish of modern interiors.

▶ **Buffet bonus**

Traditional buffets, or sideboards, are usually long and low like this one, providing plenty of storage while giving a surface area for carving and serving.

◀▼ **Swedish style**

This simple country linen cupboard, consisting of both drawers and cupboard, is painted muted gray-blue, which is very typical of the Swedish style. The robust design makes it suitable for use in the bedroom, dining area, or even the hall or landing.

▼ **Beautiful Bows**

Bow-front furniture is considered some of the finest. This triple-bow chest of drawers is particularly elegant, providing a focal point in the sitting room.

STORAGE STYLE

PERIOD DETAIL

Traditional storage built into period homes often works best when attention is paid to the detail. This does not have to be original to be in keeping, but by adding the correct casing or baseboard, it will work well within the wider architecture of the room. Lumber yards can usually run off any detail to order. Either give them a small sample of the original detail to copy, or get your architect or carpenter to draw up the required profile. As well as add-on detail, good carpenters and cabinetmakers will pay attention to the style of the glazing bars. Original Federal furniture, for example, would have had very fine frames for glass-front cabinets, some adding Chippendale chinoiserie-style diagonals.

▲ Federal finery

The glass-front cupboard set into the alcove next to the fireplace is given typical Federal style with fine diamond-style glazing bars, plus some discreet casing around the doors to match the panel molding.

▶ Niche and pretty

The niche cut into the curved wall of this Federal-style house is given period styling with a curving top that is echoed in the window treatment.

MODERN STORAGE

Modern storage tends to be understated. Its aim is to create a sleek, restrained look for a Zen-like feeling of uncluttered calm. The finer the detailing, the better, and in some cases, it is reduced to flush surfaces, devoid of even the embellishment of handles. Doors are opened using finger gaps or magnetic push-open-and-close devices. At its sparest, sliding doors disguised as walls provide cover for extensive storage, making a breeze of tidying for clear, fuss-free interiors.

Some modern furniture is also designed to handle the needs of modern technology. There is now a growing selection of living room and home office storage pieces, for example, that are equipped with specially positioned holes so that cables from media and computer equipment can be passed through and plugged into electrical outlets in the wall—both neat and efficient.

▶ Efficient simplicity

Modern island units have replaced the traditional kitchen table, combining ample storage space with a generous work surface.

▼ Light style

Here, closets have been reduced to translucent panels that screen the hanging rods. The end result is airy, but it relies on extreme meticulousness and hanging light garments, such as these white shirts, behind the panels.

FREESTANDING

Freestanding storage can be a style choice. You may, for example, have inherited a family heirloom, or found an antiques sale bargain which has developed a glorious patina that can never be reproduced on modern furniture. Beautifully made, it is difficult to find the same quality in modern furniture at an affordable price (see also pages 32–33). Many people also love the furnished look of freestanding furniture, be it antique or modern, as it offers the option of combining a useful surface with storage. This choice of storage design may also be a practical one. It's the ideal short-term solution for anyone who is likely to be on the move. Traditional furniture moved to a new residence will immediately make it feel like home, and modern pieces can provide excellent flexibility. There are many pieces designed on a modular basis, so they can easily be rearranged or added to the existing modules to fit perfectly and feel at home in their new position.

▲ **Working in style**

This pretty Louis XIV secretary makes a delightful statement in the corner of a period home, yet opens up to reveal a fully functioning workstation.

◀ **On the side**

Not all sideboards are traditional. This contemporary design introduces a light feel for today's lifestyle, combining the storage and serving surface that has made sideboards the mainstay of dining storage furniture for centuries.

◀◀ **Module makeovers**

Modern modular furniture is easy to adapt to suit both your storage needs and the space it occupies. Modules of shelves, cupboards, and drawers such as these can be rearranged and even expanded to suit new requirements.

BUILT IN

Although built-in storage is certainly not a new idea—it was often incorporated into Colonial houses—it has certainly become increasingly important in modern times. With the combination of smaller houses and generally more possessions, storage has to be ever more carefully thought out and space used to its maximum.

Built-in storage is fantastically versatile, as it offers architects and designers the potential to use otherwise dead space, filling walls from floor to ceiling with useful stowage. At the same time, it can be designed for ease of use. For instance, closets can be divided to accommodate the dimensions of actual garments, with special trouser rods and sliding pullout shelves. This principle of designing the storage for its contents can be applied to every room in the house (see the illustrated pages at the end of each room section, further on in the book).

▶ Inset storage
Delightful mesh-front cupboards set into the end wall of a kitchen make attractive and useful storage space for white china.

▼ Complementary in style
Even in old houses, built-in closets can provide efficient storage while keeping within an appropriate architectural style. Here, boarded doors with strap hinges perfectly suit this cottage bedroom with exposed beams.

OPEN SHELVING

The joy of open shelving is the light and airy feel it lends to a room. Also, items displayed on it can add a decorative element to the room, even if they're practical, such as books, or utilitarian, such as china and glass. Ranging from substantial custom-built bookshelves to simple upright-and-bracket arrangements, open shelving is also highly flexible. Even built-in shelves can be designed to be adjustable, so they can be arranged to fit their contents, which is not only more efficient, but more attractive, too. Shelves can be freestanding, built in, or fixed to the walls, using uprights and brackets, brackets on their own, or specially designed hidden features. Freestanding shelves can also be used as efficient, inexpensive room dividers to define larger spaces.

▶▲ Storage from nothing

Shelves can be used to provide storage in the most unlikely places. Here, they fill a wall, even covering the space above the window.

▶ Twice the function

Here, shelves are used as a room divider, held in place with scaffolding poles. The result is the perfect division, and it can be put to practical storage use.

▶▶ Custom fit

Bookshelves covering a whole wall, reaching even above the rafters, make highly efficient use of space without encroaching much on the overall dimensions of the room.

HIDE IT AWAY

In the interests of a neat home, many people love to hide everything away behind closed doors. It works well, so long as you have enough closets, drawers, and shelves, and they are efficiently organized to accommodate your possessions. No point in having a roomy closet fitted with a few large shelves, for example, when the small belongings you plan to store there simply end up in a jumbled mess. Alternately, divisions are no good at all if they create spaces that are too small for storing most of your things. With suitable spaces for everything, all items can quickly be put in their place. However, this program of organization will quickly fall apart when you start accumulating too many things. Once there's not quite enough space, you're tempted to cram in everything, leading quickly back to chaos. The key is to have regular (at least twice yearly) closet overhauls, when you go through and analyze what you still really want and use, and reorganize the storage to suit the new requirements.

▶ Smooth solution
Translucent glass-front cupboards provide roomy storage in the living room, the perfect cover-up for the ever-expanding media collection.

▶▲ Cover-up story
Closets lining one whole wall of this dining room make neat storage for all the requisite china, glass, flatware, and linen, leaving the space clear and tidy.

▶▶ All around
Closets lining the whole landing provide plenty of storage for towels, bedding, and linens, as well as bedroom wardrobe overflows.

SHOW IT OFF

If you love the intrinsic beauty of your possessions, you may want to enjoy them on a day-to-day basis by displaying them on open shelves or in glass-front cupboards. This does not have to be restricted to specifically decorative items or pieces of art. Everyday things, such as china, glass, bottles and jars, vases, toiletries—even shoes, hats, and stationery—can be made into great displays. If this is your style, think of the displays as part of the interior design of your home, and spend time setting them up. Put only those things you love on display, or those items that work well together. Belts and necklaces, for example, can be difficult to display attractively, in which case they are better left hidden behind doors, or they can join the display in "disguise": perhaps you could store them all together in a box, which is pretty enough to join the display.

◀ **Close at hand**

Even prosaic piles of plates and bowls can look good when gathered together on a painted shelving unit, as here. Stacked one-deep, everything is visible and you can easily retrieve what you want, but take care to keep the colors as uniform as possible.

▲ Simply stunning

Treasured collections deserve thoughtful display. These shells and sand dollars look fabulous lined up on turquoise-painted shelves. The scalloped edging around the unit serves to emphasize the collection and mimics its curvy lines.

▲ Teamwork

Possessions make more impact when they're arranged as "teams." These basic shelves make a decorative statement in a simple kitchen because all-white dishware fills most of the shelves, while a collection of turquoise soda siphons march along the top one.

EVERYTHING IN ITS PLACE

STARTING POINTS

Successful storage is much more about suiting the furniture to its contents than the other way around. Traditionally, a house was furnished with various storage systems, or with chests of drawers, wardrobes, and closets, and the homeowners had to make the best of what they had. Nowadays, there is as much emphasis on the interior accessories as there is on the furniture itself, and because of this, there is an abundance of designs to suit the various storage needs of each room. But whether or not you decide to invest in these, you can be inspired by the basic principle of dividing the space to make the most efficient use of your storage. Since each room has different requirements, the storage needs can be special to that space. The key to success, then, is to rethink all the perceived wisdom about storage and, instead, analyze exactly what you need to store in each room, bearing in mind your own particular needs.

▼ **Clever color**

The unlikely combination of books and wooden candlesticks makes a striking display because of the clever use of color, with blocks of tan and burnt sienna set against white. The sheer number of tall, spindly candlesticks along the full width of the room creates a visual impact.

◀ Modular efficiency

Modular storage with some open and some closed sections is one of the best solutions for modern living-room storage. Here, the television occupies a double module. Other sections are subdivided to create drawers and files.

◀▼ Two timing

An armoire near the dining table provides ample room for storing art and craft materials. When not used at mealtimes, the table becomes a craft bench.

▼ Pretty show

This pretty period piece provides storage for entertaining needs.

EVERYTHING IN ITS PLACE

Take the bedroom, for example. Traditionally, closets had one hanging rod at about eye level. That was perfect in the days when we wore full-length dresses and ballgowns; perhaps it's not so relevant now. Instead, you may prefer to have two hanging rods, one above the other.

Kitchens can provide another example. Until about a decade ago, all but the most upscale kitchen suppliers basically fitted boxes to walls. Most of them were cupboards, some were drawers. There were also very few internal accessories to choose from. Nowadays, you can choose roomy pan drawers, dividers that allow you to put plates in drawers, even custom-made pantries with bottle storage, wine-glass hangers, and sliding shelves. Even if you don't want to invest in custom-designed fixtures, you may still want to think through the ways you can divide your storage for greater efficiency. Shelves can be placed at the optimum distance apart to suit your book collection, items can be put into boxes appropriate to their size, then stacked on shelves for easy retrieval. All these ideas are examined in more detail throughout the rest of this book, and while the storage decision-making might not be as simple as it once was, you will find that well-conceived storage solutions pay huge dividends in terms of increased organization, efficiency, and timesaving.

▶ **Open doors**
With doors open to reveal an attractive dishware display, this period armoire combines practical storage and decorative display.

▶▶ **Custom fit**
Modern storage makes use of every available inch. Here, shelves are fixed on either side of the fireplace while a large box-like structure at the end provides overflow storage.

LIVING

display

conceal

shelves

cupboards

relaxed

personality

sorted

chests

symmetry

focus

divided

RELAXED ORGANIZATION

The living room is designed for leisure. It's the place you go when the work is done to relax with family and friends, watch TV, or listen to music. Living room storage falls into two categories: display, which brings life and personality to the interior design (see page 62), and utilitarian, encompassing the more practical elements.

Ironically, these practical elements—books, CDs, DVDs, magazines (which are designed for your pleasure)—are generally less attractive and more likely to deteriorate into a disordered mess. Not only does this look ugly, but not being able to find what you want can seriously infringe on relaxation time. The simplest solution is to hide such items behind closed doors or in drawers, but that doesn't necessarily end the problem. In the absence of order (even behind closed doors), most of these will descend into a messy heap, making finding what you need a major task. So whether you keep them on display or stowed in cupboards, CDs and DVDs must be kept in line either in holders specially designed for the purpose (see pages 64–65) or on shelves built to suit their size. It's also helpful to arrange them for easy retrieval, such as in alphabetical order or in style categories.

Traditionally, books have taken up a major part of living room storage, and if neatly arranged, their spines can bring character and color to the space, so consider organizing your books by color or size. You could also combine book storage with display. There are many ways to accomplish this. You can either simply add other items among the books or you can choose modular storage units, filling some with books and others with more decorative items to build up an interesting

▶ **Behind closed doors**

Paneled doors set into paneled walls hide abundant and practical living room storage for messy CDs, videos, and DVDs, thereby retaining the period integrity of the room. It's a simple solution that combines old-time charm with the needs of modern home entertainment.

overall display. As an alternative, choose modular units that incorporate cupboards and gather together any miscellaneous collections of books into one or more of these, leaving the open modules for more decorative display. (There is more about bookshelves in the work space section on page 150.)

A major part of living room storage is also display: it's the room where you're most likely to have your favorite paintings, photographs, souvenirs, and collections. These are an expression of you and your family; they add personality to the room and contribute to its overall interior design, depending on the way in which they are displayed. You can install shelves specially set aside for display, use tabletops or other surfaces, or use focus areas, such as alcoves, niches, or cubbyholes.

▶▲ Controlled chaos

Unless you take control of them, precious periodicals very quickly threaten to take over. Being of a uniform size, it is not too much of a problem to make them look good on display. Here, they have been piled on shelves inside a built-in cabinet for a surprisingly effective display.

▶ Pretty cabinet

Small cabinets like this one make for excellent media storage, as the scale is appropriate to the contents. This piece has been beautifully designed on clean lines, suitable for a contemporary home.

Glass-front cupboards offer storage for china and glass.

Divided into cubbyholes, this unit has innate strength and provides useful, flexible storage.

Magazine holders keep periodicals under control in one section.

Other boxes keep DVDs and CDs organized, lending an ordered look to the whole unit.

◀ **Open style**

Freestanding open shelving can provide excellent storage for open-plan living, as it can act as a room divider while allowing access to the stored items from both sides.

HOUSING THE HARDWARE

Where once the fireplace took center stage in the living room, this is now the role played by the television. And it is anything but diminishing. Add to that all the equipment of home audio and theater systems, DVD players, DVDs, and CDs, and electronics look set to take over. On the bright side bulky televisions are being replaced by flat or plasma screens, and videos by more compact DVDs.

With this dominance of technology, we're no longer apologizing for the television, hiding it in the corner or coyly behind cupboard doors. Moreover, the interior design of modern living rooms often starts with the positioning and storage of the television and all that is associated with it. This is most effective if done aesthetically, which is much easier with a sleek, flat screen in a silver housing, than it was in the days of bulky black boxes.

Inspired solutions

◆ **Audio and video** components look much neater grouped together into custom-made units designed specifically to contain each piece.

◆ **Customized television stands** often incorporate shelves for video recorders and DVD players.

◆ **Install shelves** perfectly spaced to take CDs and DVDs—in that way they're easier to keep under control.

◆ **If you don't have suitable surface space** for the television, consider a wall-mounting system. There are also mountings for speakers.

▶ **Smart geometry**
This clever modular design combines open shelves for technology storage with cupboards for DVDs, CDs, magazines, and directories. The unit makes a striking geometrical statement on one wall.

▲ **Sound solution**
Sliding doors painted to match the walls conceal a cabinet fitted with shelves designed to house the components of a sound system plus tapes and CDs.

▲ **Architectural reinvention**
Here, the mantelpiece has been adapted to accommodate much of the technology: screen below and DVD player on a shelf above.

LIVING

ON DISPLAY

Much of living room storage concerns display: the attractive arrangement of lamps, sculptures, collections, photographs, and books. For the best effect, keep the arrangement simple; a few large items will always have greater impact than lots of small ones. However, there are ways to deal with the diminutive pieces. Some, such as collections of glass paperweights that are meant for display, can be grouped for impact, giving the visual impression of one larger piece. However, not everything is beautiful in itself—magazines, CDs, and DVDs are prime examples—but that needn't prevent you from displaying them. You could, perhaps, invest in an attractive range of boxes that effectively becomes part of the display while keeping everything under control.

Displays always look best when they fill the space well; group tall items on widely spaced shelves and low items on those that are closer together. Vertically divided shelves are another key to successful display, providing cubbyholes in which you can place separate items or groups of items. These can be designed in straight checkerboard style or on a modular basis, where some compartments occupy two or more modules and other modules are subdivided. This makes it much easier to create an effective display of objects composed of disparate sizes.

Inspired solutions

◆ **Color creates extra impact.** A display using just two colors, with the addition of an accent color, will give a focal point to the whole room.
◆ **Symmetrically arranged items** always look ordered, often resulting in an elegant overall design, while asymmetrical arrangements exude design confidence.

▶ **Creative flair**
The seemingly casual arrangement of this display nevertheless betrays an accomplished eye. Books, boxes, and bowls are piled up where height is needed.

▲ **Bright solution**
Traditional library shelves painted yellow are a confident design statement in themselves, and this is reinforced by the central display of the sound system—bold and black—providing a focus for the books and possessions surrounding it.

▶ **Bold statement**
Although the sizes of the pieces in this display vary greatly, items have been displayed effectively because their sizes are linked to the height of the shelves. Each shelf is a pleasing arrangement of blue-and-white china pieces.

FINDING A BALANCE

The challenge of successful living room storage is to find a way to pair the necessity of stowing the electronics while attractively displaying all the more personal elements that bring life to the room. You can do this either by separating the elements and storing them in different units or finding ways to make them work together. Whichever you choose, it is now far easier to accommodate today's streamlined electronic gear than the bulky television sets and phonographs of 25 years ago. Even the media are neater. DVDs are so much more streamlined than VHS videos, and CDs are more easily stored than old vinyl records. Also, there are plenty of cleverly designed media storage units, some of which can also accommodate the more decorative elements of the living room, making decorating and storing so much easier.

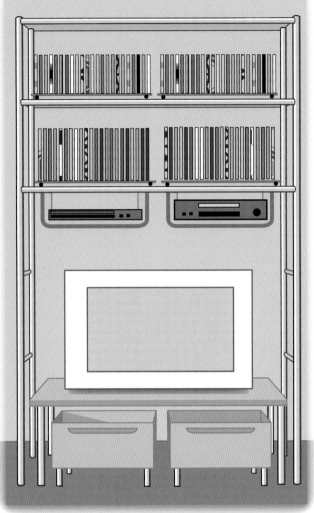

Hang it all

This clever media shelving consists of different components that can be put together to suit individual needs. The television sits on a custom-built table with room underneath for two bins. The sound system suspends neatly from the shelf above on custom-made bolted shelves, leaving plenty of room above for CD and DVD storage.

◀ Great combination

This smart modern chest offers excellent storage for the living room with plenty of space for both media storage and display. The top has been used here for showing off some favorite items, but it could equally well accommodate a flat screen television.

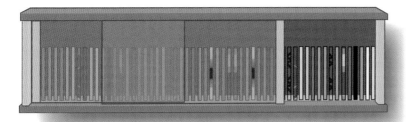

Up the wall

Here's a wall-mounted CD/DVD storage unit with sliding doors so everything can be neatly shut away. Mount it near the sound system or television so that its contents are handy.

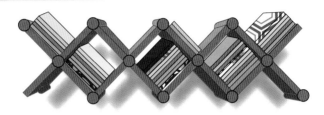

Diamond life

CD storage can be fun, providing interesting wall decoration. This diagonal module can be expanded as your collection grows for an ever-changing design.

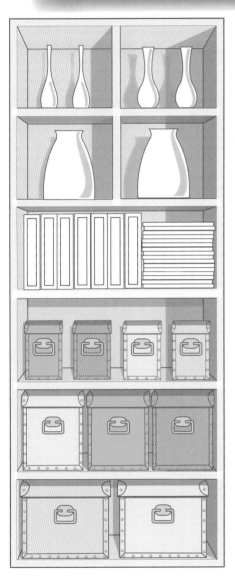

Vanishing act

Simple modular shelving is a great way to combine the beautiful with the practical. Here, some sections house displays of vases, jars, books, and magazines; others are given over to CD and DVD storage, all neatly stacked in a range of boxes.

All together now

Media storage units can be as simple as a television-size table with media-proportioned sections below, as demonstrated here. It's a neat way to keep everything under control.

Fashionable and slim

This slender storage unit with a frosted glass door offers an elegant solution for CD/DVD storage that would suit most interiors.

COOKING

efficient

tidy

flexible

decorative

hidden

pull-out

racks

jars

varied

overhead

stacked

SORTING THE SYSTEMS

The importance of careful storage planning when designing your kitchen can't be overemphasized, as it will have a huge impact on the day-to-day efficiency of food preparation and cleanup. It should be second in priority only to the work triangle that makes up the basic design of every efficient kitchen. The good news is that it is now much easier to custom design kitchen storage than ever before. While the traditional elements were designed to work with large equipment, such as stoves, dishwashers, and fridges, rather than storage needs, that is all beginning to change. Cabinetry is now produced in a greater variety of dimensions with a wider choice of dividers and inserts (see pages 74–75 and 82–83).

Once the three points of the work triangle (food preparation, food storage, washing) are established, you can begin to decide what needs storing where. Measure the dimensions of the items to be stored in each area so you can plan for the most suitable modules and shelves. So, for example, if you want a pan drawer under your cooktop, measuring will assure the correct depth for your own pans. By the same token, you can choose a slim unit with small compartments for spice and sauce jars near the stove, just where you need them when cooking.

Food storage has very different needs. Fresh food is generally stored in the refrigerator or freezer, while canned and packaged foods have, for most of the past half century, been stored in the kitchen wall cabinets,

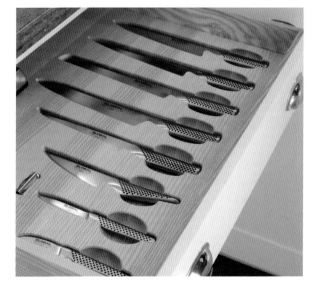

▲ Neat solution
Roomy drawers make the perfect storage solution for pots and pans in a streamlined kitchen.

▼ Big is beautiful
Drawers no longer need to be limited to storing small items. Many are made to much larger dimensions than in the past, allowing plenty of room.

▲ Mixed solution
The combination of glass-front wall cupboards and open shelving adds personality and a light and airy look to a small kitchen with solid base units. The open shelves have been reserved for holding jars of ingredients that are used every day, thereby avoiding the buildup of grease. The dishes, on the other hand, are kept clean behind glass doors.

◄ Smart multiplication
A sleek island unit doubles the storage in this well-designed Modern kitchen, making for quick and efficient cleanup. With all the modules at base level and only minimal shelving on the walls, the kitchen is kept neat and simple. The beautiful but useful items on the shelves add personality.

which replaced the traditional pantry. However, in recent years, the merits of the old-fashioned storage cupboard have been revived by specialist kitchen designers. They have taken a fresh look at the basic walk-in pantry with fixed shelves by adapting many of the shelving components designed for cabinets. By using vertical divisions and then fitting each section with a selection of sliding baskets for cans and jars, horizontal bottle storage, hanging rails for wine glasses, sliding baskets for dry storage, and vertical tray sections, a closet can be custom designed to suit your individual needs (see pages 82–83).

Many modern kitchens must incorporate storage space for china, glass, serving dishes, and a wide variety of utensils. Ideally, this space should be positioned between the sink/dishwasher and preparation/serving areas so you can put away as quickly as you can serve. Piles of plates and bowls can be decorative in themselves, and certainly add to the look of the kitchen, so some people choose to put these on open shelves or in glass-front cupboards. Open shelves are practical only for items that are used on a daily basis and are regularly washed, otherwise they develop a film of grease. However, one of the greatest advantages of shelving is that it is extremely flexible and can be cut to the perfect depth for its intended contents and spaced at the perfect distance to suit your kitchenware.

▶ **Smart practicality**

This kitchen has been designed using custom-built furniture, much of which would look equally at home in a living room. The drawers have been built into a traditional chest rather than modular style, and the cabinetwork has Georgian-style elegance. However, the glass-front wine refrigerator hints at highly practical and modern cabinet interiors.

▶▶ **Perfect combination**

Kitchen cabinets designed along more traditional lines combine the convenience of a modern kitchen with styling that suits a period home.

Glass-front cabinets provide ample storage and give an open, informal feel to the whole kitchen.

Adjustable shelving inside the cupboards allows you to fit the space to your needs.

Drawers can be fitted with modular inserts to accommodate flatware and utensils.

House all the less lovely kitchen requisites, such as measuring cups and sifters, behind solid doors.

CONVENIENT CABINETS

Cabinets custom-designed to fit the space are still the most efficient way to store the wide array of kitchen needs. But the choices have become ever more complex. While once there was a range of standard sizes, now, even within a single design, there is much more variation in the widths and heights of both cupboards and drawers. This means they can be combined in a way that meets individual needs and are more interesting to look at. Past kitchen design wisdom entailed lining every wall with base and eye-level units, and depending on the size and style of the kitchen, this can still be highly efficient. However, with the increased choice in unit sizes, there is now much more flexibility in the use of space. Modules can even be built into island units or peninsular breakfast bars, teamed with freestanding furniture or lined up just along one wall of a larger, open-plan room.

Inspired solutions

◆ **Since the style of the cabinets** will have a greater bearing on the overall look of the kitchen than any other element, this is the place to start. Choose a design that will complement the interior design of the rest of the house.

◆ **Make a list of what you wish** to store in the kitchen cabinets, along with an indication of size so that you can subsequently work out the storage that best suits your needs.

◆ **Take your time to research kitchen suppliers**— even modules at the economy end of the market usually add up to a major investment.

◆ **Take advantage of the services offered** by in-house designers who can help you plan the space to meet your needs. However, think very carefully in advance of the meeting about what you would like to include.

▶ **Flexible friends**
The greater variety in module sizes, such as these stainless-steel drawers and cupboards, not only makes for more adaptable storage, but a more interesting visual design. Here, the modules have been combined with open shelving for a charming, personalized kitchen.

◄ Country convenience

Traditional country style need not preclude modern convenience. These modular units have Georgian detailing with simple panels and understated hardware. They are in keeping with the period home into which they are built, yet offer maximum storage.

▼ Sleek solution

Modern minimalism tolerates little embellishment or display, so the solution here is to install a wall of floor-to-ceiling modular cupboards. With ample storage space, even the less neatly inclined have room to shovel everything behind closed doors for a cool, clutter-free interior.

INSIDE STORY

The art of efficient storage is to match the proportions of the shelf or drawer to that of its contents and to use every spare inch of space, accessing as many wasted corners as possible. This means you need to think of the vertical as well as the horizontal potential. Shelves need to be positioned so there isn't too much "air space" between them. The more that shelves and drawers can be divided up, the more efficiently you'll be able to find what you need, and to put it away again later.

Kitchen manufacturers have spent a lot of effort thinking through every cooking and eating storage need and are continually coming up with innovative ideas to make both the storage more efficient and people's lives easier. Many of these can be very beguiling, but they're only of use if they're really going to suit your particular needs. They can also be very expensive, so make sure it's you and not the kitchen designer who's making the decisions.

Inspired solutions

◆ **Allow yourself several visits** to the kitchen supplier. Make a careful note of the precise dimensions of the cabinet and drawer interiors, and take a snapshot, if possible. Then compare these with the items you need to store before making your final decision.

◆ **Understand how you work** in your kitchen so you can decide what kind of storage you need and where. The designer will help with the classic work triangle, but only you know how large your pans are, for example, and where you would most like to store them.

◆ **Think divide and rule** to cut down your kitchen time! A divided drawer with a place for everything and everything in its place will make finding and putting away a breeze.

▶ **Handy pans**
Generously wide drawers under the cooktop are the perfect location for pans. No fishing: just pull open the drawer and there they are, just where you need them.

▲ **The big drawer**
Plates and cups traditionally find their homes in cabinets, but stacked into wide drawers, they are much easier to handle and are probably less likely to chip. Adjustable posts can be positioned to suit the sizes of your dishware.

▲ Thin winner

Cans and jars are best stacked in one row so you can see them all at once. This narrow pullout unit is the ideal solution, making use of a spare few inches between the main storage components.

▲ Instant access

Small shelves can be just as good as drawers for compartmentalizing everyday items, especially if they are within easy reach.

◀ In position

Compartmentalize your kitchen utensils for easy access. This drawer has been divided to suit a variety of utensils and to keep them in order.

SHOW-OFFS

While minimalism might suit many people, it does not suit all; sleek, uninterrupted, wipe-clean surfaces can come at the cost of looking clinical and impersonal. There's nothing like culinary paraphernalia to give the kitchen personality and identify it as your own. However, the line between character and clutter can be a fine one, unless the kitchen is given a little order. The best solution is to display only those things whose look you love—and that can just as well be a pile of bowls or plates as your favorite casserole. After all, if you bought them for their looks, why hide them away? Whether you stack them on open shelves or behind

glass doors depends on how frequently you use them or how often you're prepared to wash them. Those that are used daily don't have time to collect the grime, but those left much longer between uses soon sport a sticky film, witness to a steamy atmosphere.

Inspired solutions

◆ **Keep shelves near** where their contents will be used.
◆ **Stack plates, cups, and casseroles** one-deep to make for easy retrieval and to avoid breakage.
◆ **Put pretty but practical plates** on display to make an attractive display that's always close at hand.

◀ New meets old

Original built-in cupboards retain the kitchen's period
character and don't look out of place, even though the
room has been updated with modern stainless-steel units.
Filled with antique dishes, this storage adds personality.

▲ Hanging display

Use hanging racks as well as shelves for storing items on
display. Here, a long rail, fixed for strength by several
brackets along its length, is the perfect parking place for
exquisite copper and stainless-steel pans.

ISLAND LIFE

With the increasing popularity of larger, more open-plan kitchens, island units have seen a renaissance. Occupying the center of the room in much the same way as the table in a traditional kitchen, they are very often the focal point. They also provide generous storage right where it's needed. Some incorporate low-level, open shelves, offering convenient storage for items such as cookbooks, breakfast cereals, and dishes. This is particularly useful if the island unit also includes a breakfast bar. Others provide space for a refrigerator, or for cabinets or drawers that harmonize with the rest of the kitchen storage units.

Inspired solutions

◆ **A counter-height** bin built under the island is excellent trash can storage, allowing you to prepare food on the worktop, then sweep the peelings straight into the trash.

◆ **With an island unit** opposite a wall-mounted row of cabinets, you can use the area like a space- and time-efficient galley kitchen, storing pans opposite the oven, for example, or dishes opposite the dishwasher.

▶ **All booked up**
Space-hungry cookbooks look less than tidy at eye level. Stacked into the side of an island unit, however, they're at hand right where you want them.

▼ **Twice as nice**
This island unit comprises a sink, preparation area, and breakfast bar, complete with two different kinds of storage, each perfectly suited to its purpose.

FREESTANDING STYLE

Before the days of built-in design, freestanding furniture dominated kitchen storage, and the cupboards of yesteryear still hold great nostalgic appeal. With open shelves above, cabinets underneath, and often a couple of drawers, they provide a flexible storage solution. Clearly at home in a traditional kitchen, they can also work well in more modern environments. There are also some kitchen manufacturers who provide units that incorporate these same elements on more updated lines. They can work very well in large, open-plan kitchens, providing a decorative element in what is often a multifunctional room. You don't have to be restricted by style. As well as classic Colonial pieces, you have the choice of pretty French armoires and antique buffets.

Inspired solutions

◆ **Use freestanding furniture** as a practical yet decorative link between the working and relaxing areas of a modern, multifunctional kitchen. A pretty, glass-front fixture, for example, housing attractive china and crystal, could look delightful in a dining or sitting area, simultaneously providing functional kitchen storage.

▶▲ Classic twist
This cupboard has been updated with a coat of off-white paint. Casseroles, jugs, plates, and bowls add a decorative touch on the open shelving, while the cabinets below provide storage for less attractive kitchen needs.

▶ Mirror image
Use freestanding cupboards to reflect an architectural element of the room. Here, a round-topped cupboard mirrors the shape of the door. It also introduces more color.

▶▶ Old charm
Original cupboards, such as this, lend character to period houses. Painted in gray-blue, typical of the Colonial period, this cabinet is the focal point of the room.

COOKING

CLEVER TRICKS

It's the secret life of kitchen storage that makes the difference between streamlined organization and chaos. It's so much easier to find and replace things if each item has its own place with everything visible. Naturally neat people are excellent at organizing their kitchen gear with large, less-used items hidden away, and jars stored in alphabetical order so there's no doubt as to what's at the back of the shelf. The rest of us owe a huge debt to those clever designers who have come up with all sorts of tricks that allow us to see everything at a glance when needed and whisk it out of the way when not. It's a winning combination: a gloriously organized kitchen with less time needed for cleaning up.

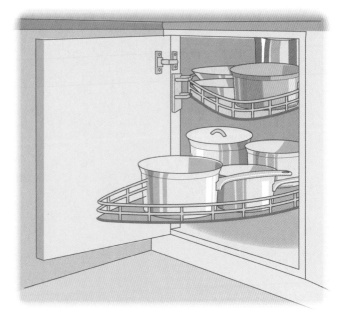

Swing-out saucepans
Bringing the problem space at the backs of corners alive, carousel units are one of the original interior gadgets. Practical and efficient, they remain among the most popular kitchen appurtenances.

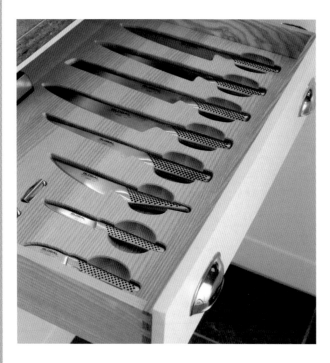

▲ Custom-made
The ultimate in organization, this drawer has been customized to accommodate a whole set of knives. In this way, it's not only easier to make your selection at a glance, but well away from other cutlery, the blades will stay sharper longer.

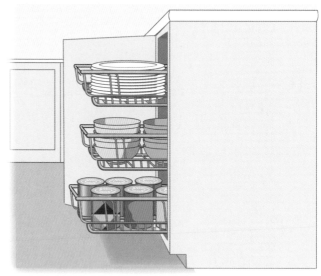

Pullout trick
Wire drawers can be used inside kitchen cupboards to store essential cooking ingredients. They create more shelf space while giving you maximum accessibility.

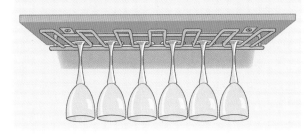

Hanging out

Make use of both sides of a shelf by storing wine glasses on racks fixed to the underside. It's an idea stolen from professional bars that works at home, too.

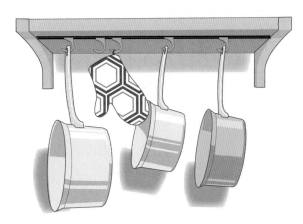

Getting hooked

A neat row of sliding hooks can be mounted under a shelf, providing an efficient solution to storing pots and pans. Choose attractive bottles and jars to store basic ingredients above the pans and position the whole arrangement near the stove for quick retrieval.

All stacked up

Built-in cubbyholes for bottles add to the kitchen design while keeping the wine in order. For other bottles, cans, and jars, built-in sliding drawers give maximum access and visibility.

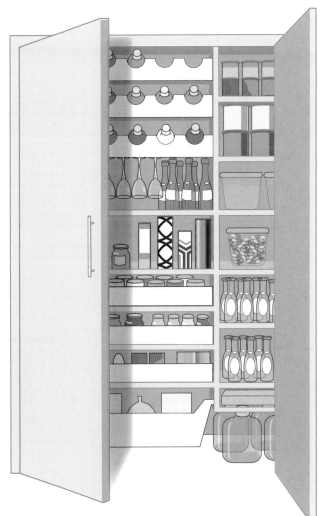

Super sorted

Custom-make yourself a perfect pantry. Closet suppliers can help you identify your needs, dividing the pantry vertically, then fitting the sections with sliding trays and baskets, hanging wine glass holders, and wine racks. Use trays or boxes for cake mixes, for instance, or for bread-making needs, and yet another for packet sauces or soups. Not only does this keep them under control, it also makes for more efficient food preparation. On a cake baking day, just take the whole tray to the preparation area.

EATING

china

glass

linens

flatware

candles

vases

buffets

cupboards

display

hidden

sparkly

TAMING THE TABLEWARE

Dining has become something of a movable feast. Modern open-plan homes are far more likely to have an eating area incorporated into the kitchen or living room than a traditional, formal dining room. This can have a bearing on how and where you position the storage, which should ideally be situated somewhere between the table and dishwashing area to make both setting up and clearing away as speedy as possible.

Ranging from neatly folded linens to large porcelain tureens, and encompassing flatware, glass, vases, and candles, without exception, dining ware looks gorgeous. This is its trump card, giving you the option of having it on display if you wish, or closeting it away behind cupboard doors for a sleeker appearance.

In the kitchen, an open cupboard, hutch, or glass-front cabinet filled with china and glass can mark a visual boundary between the cooking and eating areas. On the other hand, if your eating area is in part of the living area, or even taking up part of a connecting space, you may prefer to store the dinnerware and glassware in a closed cupboard or buffet and reserve display space for somewhat more ornamental items.

▶ Two opportunities

There are many options for tableware storage when the dining area is in the kitchen. Here cabinets are situated at both ends of the island, providing plenty of capacity just where it's needed.

▲ Neat solution

Some period homes have original built-in cupboards beside the fireplace, using the spaces that are often left as alcoves on either side of the mantelpiece. These are the perfect storage in a formal dining room.

▲ Double duty

Traditional buffets provide plenty of storage and offer a handy surface for serving. This beautiful, polished wood antique buffet has drawers for flatware and cupboards beneath for plates and glasses.

EATING

When thinking of the ideal way to store your tableware, one of the most obvious solutions is an old-fashioned, freestanding cupboard. The open shelves perfectly show off favorite china (complete with cup hooks to make best use of space), while the drawers neatly organize flatware, napkins, and candles. The large cabinets are ideal for bulkier serving pieces and stacks of plates. And you don't have to be restricted to the traditional look. The same theory can easily be transferred to modern storage systems. However, should you prefer to keep everything on display, you could choose from one of the many flatware stands now available, complete with flatware designed for hanging up.

Traditionally, tablecloths were kept in the linen closet with the bed linens, and this is still an option. However, in the interests of saving time, it is better to keep these near the rest of the tableware. One solution is to invest in some baskets in which you can keep the folded linens. Consider folding and storing them edgewise, rather than piled one on top of the other, so you can more easily take out the one you want. The same applies to napkins, though you might find it easier to put them in a smaller basket or container that is more appropriate to their size. The baskets can then be kept together on the shelf of a cupboard behind closed doors to protect them from dust and grease.

► **Artful arranging**

Stacks of china and porcelain plates, serving dishes, and cups make a delightful display on open shelves. For the ultimate in efficiency, have the shelves made to fit their contents. Here, plates are stored on the larger shelves, while teacups sit snugly on narrower, intermediate shelves. Coffee cups hung on traditional cup hooks fixed to the top shelf make even more efficient use of the available space.

◄ Fine design

Custom shelves are painted green to match the walls, making a restful background against which fine china can be displayed.

The shelves have been spaced to accommodate the various platters and serving pieces perfectly.

Open shelves can be used to store the complete dinner service, while the skilled arrangement of the individual pieces adds up to a striking display.

The glasses, which are less decorative, are neatly stacked into cupboards below.

Glass-front cupboards generally lend a lighter feel than those with paneled doors. The interiors, which have been painted to match the walls, can be seen through the panes, resulting in a cohesive décor.

◆ EATING

HUTCHES & BUFFETS

Hutches and buffets are the traditional dining room furniture. They both incorporate drawers and cupboards, but hutches usually have either open shelves or glass-fronted cupboards at the top, while buffets have a clear surface for serving. To accommodate all the tableware, at least one drawer is often divided for cutlery storage. This protects the individual pieces against damage: the best are lined with baize, a felt-like cloth that protects against the scratching of softer (and usually more valuable) metals, such as silver. However, if you still have the original boxes for valuable flatware, which provide a space for each separate piece, it is better to keep them intact and stored in an undivided drawer.

Inspired solutions

◆ **Develop your own style** by mixing and matching. Even if you have a modern home, a pretty painted antique cupboard can look exquisite set against the latest furniture lines. The key is to aim for balance in the proportions of the pieces: choose a lighter-weight cupboard to go with smaller scale or more streamlined tables and chairs, or keep to a more solid look all around, whichever best suits your style.

◆ **When buying cupboards,** measure the depth with the doors open to ensure there is enough space in your room to open them fully.

▶ Dual function

This elegant Federal-style buffet provides an excellent surface for serving and the drawers are perfect for flatware, place mats, napkins, and tablecloths. It is also the ideal place for small displays.

▶▶ Classic style

White china set against the dark wood of this Colonial-style buffet and hutch makes a striking statement in this dining room. It would look equally good in a kitchen near the eating area.

▲ Pretty as a picture

The combination of green-leaf plates and an elegant Federal-style china closet would look equally good in a period or modern home. Silver candlesticks, vases, and cruets add sparkle to this wonderful visual display that's good enough for eating areas in the toniest of living rooms.

BUILT-IN SOLUTIONS

Dining areas can be tucked into surprisingly small spaces: the table and space to pull back the chairs are the only requirements. However, storage needs can eat up floor space unless carefully planned. One solution is to plan built-in cupboards. These are especially effective if they use up nooks, crannies, and alcoves, which can be lost space, yet offer plenty of storage if outfitted with efficient shelving systems. Although wall-to-wall flush cupboards are seen as intrinsically modern, the idea of built-in is hardly a new one. Georgian houses often had walls of cupboards, though they were more likely to be paneled to blend with their surroundings. In comparison, modern styles are inclined to be flush, disguised as the wall itself. The Shakers took built-in storage to an extreme, creating floor-to-ceiling systems that incorporated cupboards and drawers of different sizes to accommodate all the needs of their communal dining. The principle of using every spare inch is highly efficient, making the best possible use of the space, while excluding dust traps that simply create more work.

Inspired solutions

◆ **When planning the system,** measure the dimensions of your own tableware so you can determine the position and dimensions of the shelves. For the depth of the shelves, measure the diameter of the plates and add an inch; for the distances between the shelves, measure the height of the stack and allow an extra six inches for lifting out.

◆ **For tureens and bowls,** create a custom-made section within the system.

▶ **All in the architecture**

Period homes often have cupboards that are built in as part of the architecture. This provides an attractive feature in the room and at the same time creates storage space that does not encroach on the floor space of the main living area.

▲ Original design

Paneled cupboards, like those below the mirror, are often built into the paneled walls of period homes. These match the internal double doors for an elegant, cohesive finish.

DOWN TO DETAILS

Most dining requisites are atractive enough to keep on display, but many of us choose to create a combination of visible and concealed storage. For the greatest efficiency, ensure you can see everything at a glance so that you don't have to waste time, for example, sorting through all the table linen before laying hands on the tablecloth cloth you're searching for at the bottom of the pile. With china and glass, having everything easily at hand is even more crucial; if the pieces are overcrowded, they're in danger of chipping or cracking as you try to wrestle them from the shelf. Tureens and serving dishes offer the greatest challenge, as they are deeper or bulkier than can usually be accommodated on regular shelves. However, if there's room, the elegant lines of a tureen can make it a focal point of display shelving, and platters can be stood up against the back of the hutch or on open shelves on special plate stands.

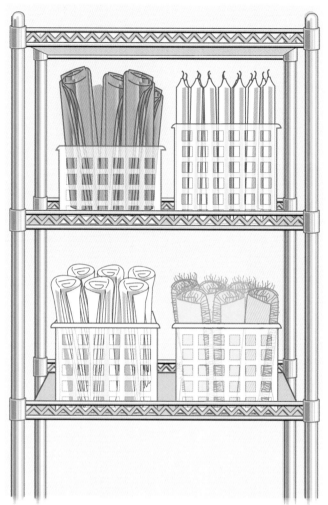

Open plan
Stainless-steel shelving units make a modern statement in an open-plan kitchen dining area. Rolled-up napkins stored in plastic crates are both convenient and attractive.

◀ Original plan
A drawer running the full width of this antique bow-front buffet was divided into capacious sections when it was built, providing plenty of storage for the full range of flatware.

Great combination

Folded tablecloths are stored vertically in baskets on the bottom shelf of this Shaker-style sideboard. Color-coordinated, it is easy to find the right one for the occasion quickly. Easy-to-grab flatware stored in a trio of mugs on the top makes an attractive display.

On display

Mug trees and flatware stands ease overcrowded cupboards and keep these everyday requisites handy on the counter.

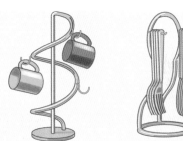

All in order

The classic buffet is excellent for dining storage. Flatware is stored in one drawer; candles and place mats in the other. Below, an adjustable metal plate-holder keeps the plates in order and protects them. Bistro glasses such as these are often designed to be stacked, making efficient use of cupboard storage. The shallow bottom shelf provides room for platters.

SLEEPING

decorative

efficient

planning

customized

hanging

shelves

shoe racks

accessories

rods

fitted

armoires

CLOTHES UNDER CONTROL

Bedroom storage demands are exceeded only by those of the kitchen. As well as clothes, shoes, and accessories, you must store spare bedding, toiletries, and medicines, and possibly even luggage. Although the traditional solutions of freestanding wardrobes and chests of drawers make a delightful contribution to the interior decoration of the room, they are not always the most efficient. Lately, bedroom storage has learned a lot from kitchen design, borrowing many of the cleverest ideas for closet interiors from its culinary cousin.

When thinking about bedroom storage, plan the space to fit its contents to make use of every spare inch. You also need to take into account what sort of person you are. Do you derive satisfaction from neat piles of beautifully folded sweaters, or does that ultimately irritate you because the minute you pull one out, the whole stack gets jumbled? Maybe you're the sort who loves to see everything hanging up on its own hanger, preferably color coordinated for easy selection. By considering these two questions, you can decide if you're a hanging rod person or a shelf person, and so plan for how much you need of each.

Start with the rods. Do you need full-length hanging space or half height? You may decide that with just one or two full-length dresses or gowns, you can forego full-height hanging altogether. Expensive dresses are

▲ Under control

Piles of clothes are much easier to control when the shelves are sectioned off and set fairly close together, allowing one manageable pile for each cubbyhole. That way, if one section becomes disrupted, all is not lost.

◀◀ Paint style

Painted pine chests bring color to the room and can be repainted as needed or to keep up with changing fashions in interior décor.

◀ All in order

A small cupboard offers the ideal solution for the essential creams, lotions, and potions that tend to crowd bedroom tabletops.

best dry cleaned after use, then stored carefully folded into boxes lined with acid-free tissue paper. These can then occupy top-shelf space. The length of rod you need depends on whether you're a folder or a hanger. Consider your partner's needs, too. Maybe you'd like two rods each, hung one above the other. Or perhaps you would prefer a top rail for shirts and a special pull-out trouser hanger unit (see pages 104–110).

When it comes to the shelving there are many options. Chests of drawers are essentially pullout shelves. However, apart from the fact that some can be divided for accessories, they offer little flexibility. Modern bedroom closet inserts, on the other hand, can offer adjustable fixed and pullout shelving, close-set pullout shelves for single shirts, shelf dividers, pullout boxes, and shoe racks (see pages 106–110).

For planning your shelving needs, begin with shoes. These will have a much longer life if given a little room to breathe, rather than left in a heap at the bottom of the closet. Determine the space yours require, then decide how best to accommodate them. There are many ways to store accessories, ranging from tie racks to stacking boxes on shelves (see pages 108–111). Many specialty suppliers also install convenient storage solutions behind period-style doors, offering the best of modern storage while maintaining the integrity of the older home.

▼ Big winner

Generously proportioned chests incorporating drawers of various sizes make for highly efficient storage. Larger items, such as sweaters, can be kept in the big drawers, while smaller drawers can be divided for accessories.

◀ **Great combination**
This 1930s-style chest of drawers is made from polished wood. The stone top adds a practical touch: It is far more resilient than wood and won't mark if anything wet or hot is put on the surface.

A miniature chest of drawers provides the perfect storage for smaller items, such as handkerchiefs, jewelry, and makeup.

The top drawer in a traditional chest is very often the shallowest, suitable for smaller items such as socks, tights, belts, and underwear. For updated organization, fit these with drawer dividers, such as those shown on page 108.

The lower drawers become progressively deeper. This is not only visually more pleasing, it helps improve stability, especially when the drawers are opened.

ALL TUCKED IN

Wardrobes, armoires, and chests of drawers are the backbone of bedroom storage, adding an elegant furnished look to the room. In the eighteenth and nineteenth centuries, the tendency in grander homes was to make the body of the piece from an inexpensive soft wood that was usually veneered to match the polished mahogany drawer and door fronts. Less expensive pieces, made entirely of pine, were often painted. In Sweden, though, even the grandest homes were furnished with painted furniture. In the United States the predominant style depended on the ethnicity of the settlers. Whatever its provenance, an elegant curved front and detailing witnessed to the best of quality.

Inspired solutions

◆ **Antique wardrobes, armoires, and linen cupboards** were usually outfitted with shelves or hooks, but these can be replaced with rods. Where a wardrobe is equipped with an original rod it is likely to run from front to back because most lack the depth to hold hangers the other way. Take a hanger with you when buying.

◆ **Check how the drawers work** before buying. Damaged or warped runners can mean they'll never open and close easily. If there's no damage, rubbing a candle or beeswax over the runners will help.

▲▶ Ultimate elegance

The graceful lines of this most unusual linen cupboard would look exquisite in any style of room.

▶ Winning color

Antique armoires such as this have a grandeur that is hard to match. This combination of palest gray plus blue would work well in many interior schemes.

▶▶ Scandinavian classic

The gray-blue paint on this delightful double-bow chest is typical of eighteenth-century Sweden. It's a look that has lost none of its charm over the years.

EQUIPPED FOR EFFICIENCY

The dual trends of smaller bedrooms in modern homes and more sophisticated space planning in modern architecture have given rise to efficient, fully equipped storage for bedrooms. Closets are fitted with rods, compartments, shelves, and cubbies that are designed for specific contents, making it easier to see and find what you need. And it makes straightening up so much easier, too. Today, there are many bedroom storage specialists, those in traditional design and manufacturers' showrooms, and those doing business strictly on the Internet. They can help you analyze and plan exactly what you need, supplying both the practical interiors and wide ranges of door designs, so there will be something for everyone.

Inspired solutions

◆ **The more you plan** before you meet the suppliers, the more successful the outcome will be. As well as the possessions you plan to store, you need to think about your lifestyle.

◆ **Think about the hanging rods** you want. How much full-length hanging do you really need? Would you be better off with two half-height ones, stacked one above the other?

◆ **Check out any special inserts.** For example, will you find it more convenient to hang trousers on a special pullout rack, or do you prefer traditional hangers? Would you prefer to have neatly pressed shirts on shelves or keep them hidden in drawers?

▶ **One at a time**
If space allows, one shirt per cubby is best for a quick early morning turnaround; they're all easy to see. It's also a breeze for keeping neat, as pulling out one doesn't disturb the rest. Straightening up is easy, too, because you simply put each freshly laundered and folded shirt into its own compartment.

▲ Great planning

Well-planned closet interiors are made to fit their contents. Here, two rods offer plenty of hanging space, and the shelves are divided to accommodate each pair of shoes and folded work shirts perfectly. With one cubicle per pair of shoes, footwear is easy to select. Choosing more low-height shelves than tall ones makes it easier to keep folded garments under control.

◀ Organized life

Color-grouped clothes, both hanging and folded, make for perfect, easy-find storage. For most of us, a few more divisions might be easier to cope with.

SHOE SOLUTIONS

Unless they're kept in order, shoes very quickly jumble into a mess at the bottom of the closet, losing their partners, as well as their shine and shape. Ideally, each pair should have its own reserved place to which it returns every night, preferably kept in shape by shoe trees. Pair-size cubbyholes offer the ultimate solution, but this can seriously eat up closet space. However, shoe-depth shelves will be a little more economical on space, accommodating two, three, or more pairs of shoes. Another solution is to buy special see-through shoe boxes that can be stacked either on shelves or at the bottom of the wardrobe. More economically, you can keep the boxes that the shoes were sold in. Many have a label at one end with a picture of the shoes, which is helpful when selecting.

Inspired solutions

◆ **Women's designer shoes** are often virtual sculptures in themselves, and can be put on display shelving or racks, bringing personality to the room.

◆ **Special canvas shoe holders,** designed with integral hooks to hang on the back of the door can make use of unused space.

◆ **Categorize your shoes** when storing them, putting sports shoes, day shoes, and evening shoes on different shelves.

◆ **Little-used evening shoes** can be stored together in a larger box at the back of the closet.

▶ **Tall storage**
Shoe-depth shelves each have space for three pairs of shoes. Grouped according to color, they're easy to find and put away. Taller ankle boots fit two pairs to the shelf when stored on their sides.

▲ Transparent protection

Special see-through stacking boxes make ideal shoe storage, as they use less space than shelves designed for just one row of shoes. Shoes should be thoroughly dry before storing.

▼ Measure for measure

It's not unusual for well-stored shoes to take up to half the closet, which is why it's a good idea to accurately assess your needs before going to the closet supplier. That way, they can design to meet your individual specifications.

ACCESSORIES UNDER CONTROL

Bags, belts, scarves, and caps all need their space, but being of such diverse shapes and sizes, storing them is never as straightforward as the basics. The solution for successful storage is to match the storage to the items. So, hang up anything that can be hung, such as bags, ties, or necklaces; roll up anything that can be rolled, such as belts, socks, or tights, then tuck them one-deep in a shallow drawer. There are also many clever drawer dividers designed specially for smaller accessories, such as underwear and tights. Inserted into the drawer like a drawer liner, they offer one section per item, thereby keeping everything under control. Another idea is to buy boxes or baskets, one per type of accessory, and just toss them in. Not such a good idea for items that tangle easily, such as necklaces, but excellent for paired socks and rolled-up tights.

Inspired solutions

◆ **Mount hooks** on the inside of closet doors to hang scarves for easy accessorizing when putting together your outfit.

◆ **Hats need extra protection** so store them in boxes or on individual hooks.

◆ **Gather together related cosmetic products,** such as nail polish, remover, and cotton balls, in an attractive box. That way, they can be stored away or left on display on an open shelf or chest of drawers.

◆ **Store jewelry** according to size in different boxes: chokers in one, long necklaces in another, and bracelets and bangles in a third.

▶ **Divide and conquer**

These divided drawers are the perfect solution for all accessories. The narrow compartment in the front used for rolled-up belts could just as effectively store rolled-up ties. The larger sections behind are good for T-shirts, pajamas, or underwear.

▲ **Boxed in clever**

These original Victorian hatboxes would look exquisite on a bedroom shelf. They needn't be restricted to holding hats; they'd also be good for handkerchiefs, underwear, tights, and gloves.

▲ Bags of style

Evening bags are so pretty in themselves that they can be kept on display. Here, two rows of white-painted peg rail hung with delightful beaded and embroidered bags make a charming display.

▲ Hang it all

Parallel poles are a clever way to store scarves and wraps, making an attractive patchwork of color in an alcove, while offering a good view of each garment. Use simple wooden dowels or adapt metal towel racks. By color-coordinating the wraps, you can turn this practical storage into a vibrant display.

WINNING COMBINATIONS

Clever clothes storage depends more on what goes on inside the closet than on the shape and size of closet itself. Put simply, the more your wardrobe is divided up, the more easily you will be able to store and find your clothes. They're also more likely to stay hung or folded up properly, which is likely to prolong their useful life. There is a growing army of closet accessory manufacturers, all of whom provide a wide choice of clever dividers and inserts designed to fit into the sides of closets or clip onto shelves. Look for trouser hangers, tie racks, shelves with ready-made dividers, and shoe racks. Alternatively, you can instantly customize the closets you already have with clip-on shelf dividers or drawer dividers made of canvas, or even cardboard. Another solution is to invest in some storage boxes to use as catch-alls for smaller items.

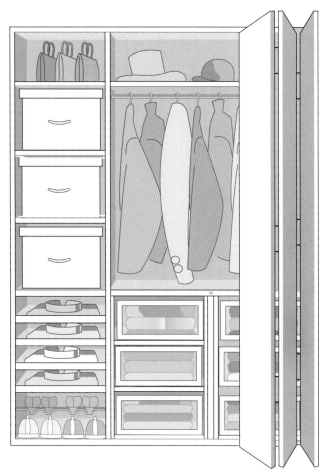

Property divided

Lack of space doesn't mean you can't be on top of things. Fit the narrowest of closets with folding doors for slim-line opening, then choose space-saving organizers for the interior. This closet features narrow sliding shelves for shirts and translucent drawers for T-shirts and sweaters. Boxes on shelves house accessories like socks, tights, lingerie, and handkerchiefs.

◄ All at hand

Handbags can add a decorative touch to the bedroom when hung one to a hook on a spare wall. Besides, you'll be able to see them all at a glance, so no more rummaging for them at the bottom of the closet.

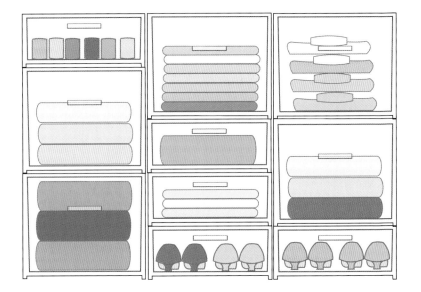

Great divisions

No space for storage? These stackable Plexiglas boxes with drawer fronts come in a variety of sizes perfect for shoes, shirts, and sweaters. Build a wall of them, allowing a place for everything to make it easy to find and return each item.

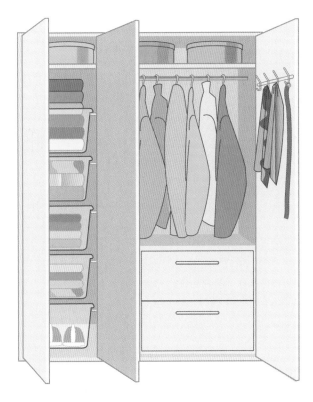

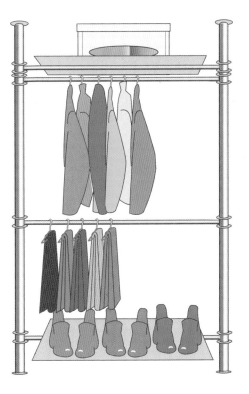

All-in-one

Keep all your clothes in one place, both to save space and to help with quick dressing. A set of door hooks for scarves and belts allows for instant accessorizing. Keep bulkier items in the drawers below. Sliding boxes are great for storing hair dryers and lingerie; use dividers in drawers for smaller items.

Out in the open

Not all clothes storage has to stay in the closet. A system of poles with shelves, drawers, and shoe racks that clamp on scaffold style can be the perfect solution for organized people. This one features (from bottom), a shoe rack, trouser hangers, a hanging rod, and top shelf with boxes for socks and underwear.

CHILDREN'S CHANGING NEEDS

It's difficult to imagine when decorating the nursery what your five-, ten-, or even fifteen-year-old will need. Although you may have moved at some point before their teens, it's worth bearing in mind that their needs will change fairly dramatically about every five years from birth to leaving home. From an organizational point of view, the nursery needs to be designed to suit your needs, rather than the child's. You're unlikely to leave your toddler on her own for any length of time, except when she's asleep. She's much more likely to play during the day around your routine, so you'll need to accommodate big toddler toys somewhere in your living/cooking area.

From about five years old, however, she'll spend more time in her own room, and this is when you need to start teaching a little rudimentary picking up.

Youngsters love sorting, so make sure there are plenty of crates and boxes of differing sizes into which the different toys can be sorted: farm animals in one, for example, building blocks in another. Toys generally get smaller as children get older, which is fortunate, as they also multiply at an alarming rate, so keep reassessing the storage boxes you need, relating them to the size of the toys. While the children are still young, they are most likely to do arts and crafts with you in the kitchen (see page 154), but as they reach around ten years old, they may want a desk in their bedroom, both for schoolwork and for creative projects.

By the time they reach their teens, the younger members of the family may well have their sights set on the largest bedrooms in the house as their needs expand into a bedroom work studio.

▶ **Shared resources**
Shared rooms make the best use of space when all the storage is kept together, though it's best to divide it into separate areas for each child. Here, the central closets separate the two sets of bunks, and generous under-bed drawers offer additional storage.

◀ **Separate arrangements**

Where teens share a room, separate pieces of furniture are probably the wisest option. These twin girls each have a generous chest of drawers plus two sections of the wall-hung magazine rack.

▼◀ **Diapers on display**

The nursery needs to be inviting and stimulating for the baby, but when it comes to storage, it's Mom who must be pleased. Gingham-lined baskets make pretty storage for all the diaper needs. Choose large baskets for the diapers themselves, smaller ones for powders and creams.

◀◀ **Reaching the heights**

Planning children's closets is much the same as for adults, but with smaller-scale clothes, you need less space. When they're babies and don't need to be able to reach, you can install three stacked hanging rods, as here. For older children, keep everything they need within reach and use top shelves for spare bedding or out-of-season garments.

CONTROLLED CHAOS

Few children are naturally tidy, and keeping track of toys is one of a mother's challenges, even as she attempts to teach the rudiments of organization. The key is to have a place for everything and get everything back into its place at bedtime. This is much easier if your child can get the big cars back into their big box while you sort the little ones, or you can both do building blocks together. Match the size of the box to its contents and the boxes to the shelves on which they sit. Generally, as the child's dexterity improves, the toys get smaller until, by the time they are around seven years old, cars are micro and dolls are miniature, so smaller containers have to be deployed.

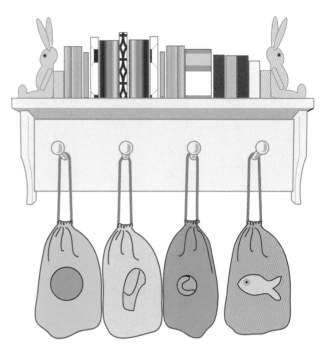

Get hooked

Right from the first football practice or ballet lesson, hunting for the backpack becomes a routine challenge. So provide a bag for each activity and keep all the related items together in it. Hung one to a hook, they'll be easy to find when needed. The shelf also provides storage for books and toys.

▲ Double the fun

House-shaped hanging wall shelves are divided up to take a variety of toys, providing display and storage space at the same time.

Swingin' softies

Soft toys multiply faster than rabbits. Keep them under control by storing them in their own hammock hanging over the child's bed.

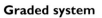

Graded system

Carefully planned shelving can accommodate a surprising number of toys. Put the biggest toys in the largest boxes at low levels, stacking gradually smaller boxes holding finer and more detailed toys farther up. Tiny tubs at the top of these shelves are easy to reach and, filled with little light items, won't do any harm if they fall.

Stacked solution

Sometimes it's a good idea to store related toys separately but keep the containers close to each other. Here, the action figures live in one box, stacked on top of another container filled with other toys, while baby dolls in a third box are stacked on top of a crate containing their clothes and equipment.

Wheelie useful

Brightly colored containers in a wheeled unit make for quick pick-up, while the lion, elephant, and monkey are fun additional storage ideas.

BATHING

display

secret

freestanding

hideaway

built-in

splashproof

small

neat

modular

vanity unit

cubbyhole

BATHROOM STORAGE

When it comes to looks, bathroom essentials range from some of the prettiest items in the house to some of the drabest. You can show off the beautiful: lovely bottles of bath products and cleansers, luxury soaps, pretty perfumes, clouds of cotton puffs, and piles of fluffy towels. However, it's best to plan to hide not-so-lovely deodorants, sanitary items, razors, toothbrushes, and toothpastes, while for safety's sake, you'll need to keep medicines and chemicals such as tub and toilet cleaner locked away out of the reach of young hands.

The first step is to decide how many (if any) open shelves you'd like, which will depend on what you'd like to have on display. A few perfume bottles can add a decorative element to the bathroom, and will require just a couple of glass display shelves, for example, whereas piles of towels will need larger spaces, such as tiled cubbyholes that may be an intrinsic part of the architecture. Between those extremes, you can plan for simple mounted shelves, or invest in freestanding units that could be either wooden or metal. Items can be stored directly on shelves or within water-resistant containers made of plastic or metal.

However, even if you do like the look of open shelving, you're likely to need at least some closet space, if only for medicines. If you're at the stage of planning the bathroom, bear in mind all the paraphernalia you may like to stash away, and plan for more than you think you could possibly use. As well as the more obvious bathroom requisites, you'll need space for spare toilet paper rolls, seasonal items such as suntan lotions, a first-aid kit, loofahs, back brushes, and beauty preparations, for example.

▶Slick pair
This wall-hung cabinet with inset steel sink makes a subtle architectural statement, especially when teamed with its coordinating mirror, and it provides plenty of the necessary storage space.

◀ **On display**
Simple glass shelves make an elegant display area in this chic modern bathroom. Shelves to the left have been used for towel storage. With two sets of feature shelves, the more practical storage can be kept hidden behind flush doors.

There are many products that are beautifully packaged and deserve to be shown off. An alcove fitted with glass shelves is the ideal situation for them.

A narrow shelf above the basin makes ideal storage for shaving mugs, soaps, toothbrushes, and decorative items.

Towels eat up storage space, but stacked on shelves in the bathroom, they're ready where they are needed. Stack them in coordinated groups with the largest fold outward.

BATHING

Bathroom cabinets probably have the greatest influence on the style of the room. Contemporary bathrooms often incorporate some kind of vanity unit. These range from neo-Victorian washstand styles, which look good with period cast-iron, claw-foot baths through twentieth-century units with inset or semi-inset sinks to modern fuss-free cabinets with bowls. However, some ultramodern bathrooms have closets that are so discreet, they're hidden behind mirrors (see pages 124–125) or disguised to look like paneled walls with handle-free, touch-open doors. This frees up the design for a more freestanding than built-in look with sinks that are almost Zen-like: round, square, or oblong and set on a simple workbench-like structure. These designs often have coordinating freestanding furniture, such as drawer modules and low tables that can be positioned under the workbench.

If you're beyond the planning-from-scratch stage, and you feel the storage space is limited, there is still a lot you can do to expand. There's a wide choice of freestanding bathroom storage furniture, some of it on wheels, some made to be mounted on the wall, and some designed for display. There are also general freestanding storage units that are ideal for stowing various bathroom needs.

▶ **Bedroom inspired**
This vanity unit took its inspiration from a traditional dressing table with drawers at either end. It provides excellent storage space for the many small items that need to be stored in the bathroom.

▶▶ **Freestanding style**
Sinks supported by metal frames like this lend a light and airy feel to the bathroom, but lose out against vanity units in terms of integral storage. The solution here is to use a period armoire, which provides plenty of storage space and at the same time adds style to the room.

GORGEOUS SHOW-OFFS

So many bathroom necessities are beautiful that it's a shame to hide them away. Exquisite bottles deserve to be displayed, as do attractive soaps, prettily packaged perfumes, and pure bristle shaving brushes. Towels can make very different, but equally striking displays, especially if neatly folded. This is not a new idea, but more contemporary bathrooms often incorporate bench-like furniture that suits larger storage, such as towels, which can bring vibrant color to the bathroom. Whatever the shelving is used for, it should always be made from water-resistant material. Metal and glass are the more obvious solutions. Alternatives are tiled, mirrored, or wooden shelves painted with oil-based or similar paint, or even wood treated with linseed oil, which is surprisingly resilient to water.

Inspired solutions

◆ **Build up a collection** of favorite antique or ultra-modern glass bottles and fill them with your favorite lotions and potions.

◆ **Mount glass shelves** in front of mirrors to reflect and double the effect of the display.

◆ **Even some of the more practical** bathroom necessities can be attractive arranged in a series of wide-mouth glass jars, then set in a row on a shelf. One jar could hold cotton balls, another, wrapped soaps, and a third, rolled face cloths.

◆ **A shelf next to the bath** is useful for storing decorative but practical objects. Less beautiful items, like shampoos and conditioners, can still look reasonably good if kept in order in attractive, waterproof baskets.

◀ Right there

Glass shelves set against black tiles and filled with an array of bottles and jars add a decorative element to a tiny bathroom. Arranging items in a single row makes it easy to find what you need.

▲ Open style

Modern bench sink units like this one provide plenty of low-level storage for larger items, such as towels. Carefully folded and organized, they can contribute to the overall design of the bathroom.

CONCEALED STORAGE

There's a lot to fit into a modern bathroom, yet it is often allocated one of the smallest rooms in the house. This shouldn't pose too much of a problem for a good designer, but there is always the danger that the bathroom could begin to look cluttered.

One solution is to keep the surfaces free and aim for maximum storage space behind sleek doors for a clean, restful look. Purist modern architects favor totally flush doors, free even from visible hinges and handles, to disguise them as wall panels or mirrors. To meet this demand, designers have come up with a variety of ways to open the doors, including bottom-edge finger holes and magnetic touch mechanisms. From a practical viewpoint, concealed storage works well in bathrooms because the plumbing fixtures and their connections at low level allow plenty of room for cabinets above. Even if the cabinets are somewhat shallow, it's not a problem: few bathroom essentials need deep shelves, and stored one-deep, everything is visible and handy. The beauty of concealed storage is that lots of toiletries can be shoveled behind the doors for an instantly tidy look.

Inspired solutions

◆ **In bathrooms** you can make use of even the smallest nooks and niches, as there are many little items, such as dental, shaving, and makeup accessories that need shelf space. Flush doors transform a space into a closet into which everything can be swept away and hidden from sight.

◆ **As well as providing extra storage,** flush doors can be used to "smooth out" niches and create a more sleek overall look, and a greater sense of space.

▶ **Spacious closets**

Even traditional bathrooms can employ concealed storage. Here, mirrored doors open up to reveal abundant storage space for towels, toilet paper, and spare bedding.

▲ Clear leader

All the closet space in this circular bathroom is concealed behind what looks like the walls, fitted flush with the cabinet under the sink. With everything hidden away behind closed doors, the bathtub can take the lead role in a minimalist bathroom.

▲▲ Illusion of space

What appear to be ordinary bathroom mirrors are actually doors that open to reveal ample storage space just where you need it, above the sink.

FREESTANDING STORAGE

While many bathrooms are designed around stream-lined built-in modules, others aim for a more furnished look, in keeping with the rest of the house. Original Victorian bathrooms were equipped with freestanding pieces, but with the coming of the Modern movement, much of twentieth-century bathroom design was built in. By the end of the century, with the blossoming of an interest in period houses, Victorian-style bathrooms enjoyed renewed popularity. With this interest, combined with the popularity of Zen-style interiors, and possibly a reaction against built in, bathrooms are again enjoying more of a furnished look, with sinks either set into or surface-mounted onto what looks like a piece of furniture. Technically, of course, these aren't truly freestanding as the sink requires attached plumbing. However, if there is room, any stand-alone piece of storage furniture, such as a chest of drawers or small cupboard, can be used in the bathroom, which invariably adds charm and personality to the space.

Inspired solutions

◆ **Any piece of furniture** that is large enough to incorporate a sink can be adapted to become a vanity unit. Choose a sink that allows enough clearance front and back. If you want surface-mounted taps, check that there is sufficient room for them, too, before buying. If in doubt, ask the retailer. All sink stands should come with a template for the carpenter or stonecutter to use when cutting the hole.

◆ **Bear in mind** what you want to store when buying. Many bathroom necessities are small, so you may prefer a piece of furniture with lots of tiny drawers and compartments to fewer, roomier shelves.

▶ **Period inspiration**
Inspired by a Victorian combination of a chest of drawers and washstand, this piece of furniture perfectly suits the attic room in which it is set.

▲ **Mirror, mirror**
A pair of Thirties-style mirrored chests, each fitted with a sink, makes a dramatic statement and reflects the light to brighten the whole room.

▶ **New for old**
A bathroom with all the conveniences of modern living—and an abundance of lovely storage space—can still retain a sense of traditional style. Here, a large cupboard fills the area beneath the sink. Its traditional finish is offset by its contemporary design.

CLEAR ORGANIZATION

The triple concerns of organized bathroom storage are the shortage of space, the need to keep lots of small articles under control, and the safekeeping of medicines. Any form of bathroom storage should address the first two concerns, and you need at least one piece to address the last, especially if you have a young family.

Each storage unit needs to be space conscious and ideally subdivided to accommodate myriad small items. You may buy a storage unit that comes divided, providing lots of small drawers or shelves. If you prefer the look of a larger, sleeker piece of furniture, be it built in or freestanding, you can always invest in a collection of boxes or baskets that can be used to separate the bathroom essentials. This not only keeps them under control, it also reduces the cluttered effect of bathroom storage, which is particularly important if everything is on display.

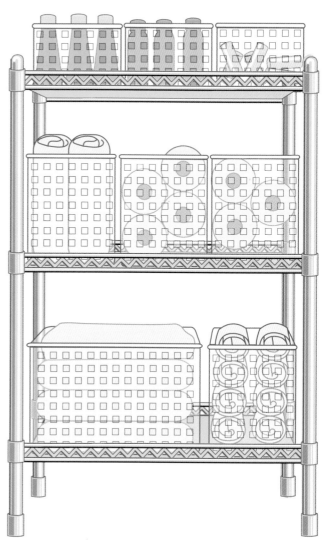

Mix and match

A collection of plastic baskets can be the key to bathroom storage. Here, different sizes of the same style of basket create a cohesive look, though they are used to accommodate a very disparate group of items, ranging from large bath towels to cosmetics. Stacked on steel shelves, they make an eye-catching display. Use the same idea to organize the shelves in your bathroom closet.

◀ On display

Glass shelves at the end of the tub can be dedicated to the decorative display of beautifully packaged bath products, or you can use them for more practical purposes, such as towel storage—just where you need it.

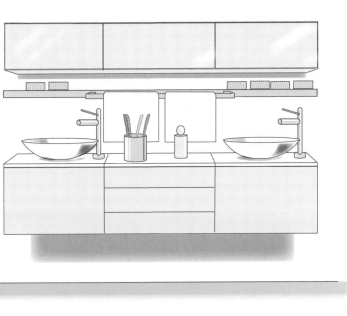

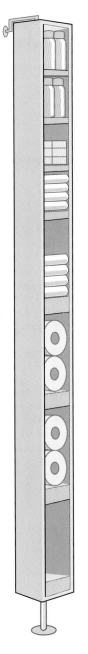

New looks

Wall-mounted cupboards with surface-mounted sinks create a contemporary look. This module incorporates two cupboards and three drawers, while the over-sink rack makes the perfect place to keep hand towels. Medicines can be kept in the top mirrored cupboards.

Tall story

This tall, thin shelving unit is ideal in the bathroom where space is at such a premium; It is a particularly clever design, as you can use the unit open-faced, or simply rotate the unit for a neat cover-up.

On the move

This portable freestanding chrome bathroom caddy not only looks good, it's practical, too. It can be kept in a roomy shower yet be readily moved to the bath area when needed.

Furnished flexibility

Suspended counters offer a clean, modern look to the bathroom, which the latest designs are pairing with freestanding pieces of furniture, such as this chest. It combines an unstructured look with more flexible storage, as it can be kept in any part of the room.

CONNECTING SPACES

slim

niche

sleek

console

hooks

hat stands

welcome

peg rail

hidden

secret

STOLEN SPACES

Halls, stairways, and landings are generally given no more space than is absolutely necessary, as these are passageways, rather than living spaces. However, it is surprising how much space can be stolen from these areas for storage. Quite apart from the obvious under-stair spaces, which can be transformed into storage areas, there are often spare inches along the sides of corridors that can be turned into closets. Fitted with floor-to-ceiling shelves, you'll be amazed at how they add up in terms of square footage for storage. For the best possible use, as always, design to fit the storage to suit the contents. For example, make sure the shallow broom closet on the landing is deep enough for the vacuum cleaner, and you should be able to fit in everything else you need. At the top, attach brackets for hanging each broom, brush, and vacuum hose to keep everything snug against the wall above the space occupied by the vacuum itself.

Any narrow shelving works well in connecting spaces, making this a great place to accommodate what always seems to be an ever-increasing population of books.

The one storage necessity in or near the entry hall or back door is for coats, hats, outdoor shoes, and umbrellas. Most of these are bulky, untidy items, so it's best to hide coats and rainboots, at least, away under the stairs or in a closet. Hats, scarves, and umbrellas can be decoratively controlled in a hat or umbrella stand near the front door where they are needed. The other hallway staple is a table, which is not only an extremely useful piece of furniture, but designed on narrow lines to fit into confined spaces, it can single-handedly give a well-furnished look to the hallway.

▲ **Versatile drawers**
A landing can be the perfect place for installing large quantities of storage space. Here, banks of drawers and cupboards are tucked into a recess.

▲ **Lateral thinking**
Here, a large, beautiful shell serves as both an accent piece and a safe, convenient container for keys by the front door. Limited space? Think outside the box.

◄ Light solution
This second-hand dresser was given a pleasing ecru lacquer finish that makes perfect sense in the hallway. Its glossy surface is easy to wipe clean in this heavy traffic area, and it lends a sophisticated air to the whole space.

A neat tray on top of the hall chest is the perfect parking place for the day's mail.

Hallways are often the gloomiest spot in the house, but the pale shiny finish of this chest considerably brightens the space.

Accommodating eight drawers, this chest is the ideal hallway solution where a huge variety of everyday paraphernalia is habitually dropped onto any available surface. With a choice of drawers, there's ample space to divide up and tidy away keys, fold-up umbrellas, scarves, and bags.

OUTDOOR ACCOMMODATION

When coming home wet, dusty, or even sandy, it's nice to have somewhere near the door to stow outdoor garments and footwear that you'd rather not bring into the main part of the house. Hat and umbrella stands have their own appeal, often designed as decorative pieces of furniture in themselves. From a practical point of view, umbrella stands also protect the floor, having a tray to catch dripping raindrops. Coats are more of a problem because they're bulky and not particularly welcome left hanging around the hallway. The best solution is to hide them away in a closet or under the stairs, if such space is available.

If you don't have closet space, there are alternative solutions: the classic Shaker peg rail is predictably practical, spreading the coat load while helping air out the garments. There is also the need in some homes for space to put mucky outdoor shoes, such as gardening and athletic shoes, riding boots, and sailing shoes. If there is a back entrance or front porch, these are the obvious spots. If not, a shallow closet, fitted with cubbyholes designed to accommodate each pair of footwear is the best solution.

Inspired solutions

◆ **Look for hidden spots,** such as in niches, behind supporting pillars, or short returns on staircases to site narrow hall or landing closets. That way, they won't hinder circulation of traffic.

◆ **Turn the necessary** into the decorative by hunting in antique markets for beautiful hat and coat stands that will make a statement in the hallway.

◆ **Invest in some good-looking hangers,** as they help keep garments (especially wet ones!) in shape. They can also help transform what looks like an untidy mess into something with more structure and appeal.

▲ **Neat feature**
Making use of what might be wasted space in the dog-leg of the stair, this custom-built storage unit is ideal for colorful sailing and swimming gear.

▶ **Shaker solution**
A Shaker-style peg rail makes the ideal solution for accommodating the family coats in a traditional farmhouse, at the same time providing space under the coats for riding boots.

CONNECTING SPACES

THE LINEN CLOSET

Upper landings make a great place for the linen closet, ideally placed in easy reach of the bedrooms and bathrooms. Traditionally, sheets, pillowcases, tablecloths, and napkins were stored in a linen press, which is a cupboard furnished with plenty of shelves to keep everything in order. Quilts and blankets were kept in blanket chests, often at the end of the bed. We still need to store quilts, comforters, and pillows for winter months or for when guests come to stay; if we have neither the space nor inclination to keep a blanket chest in the bedroom, space will need to be found in the linen closet for these, too. They're bulky items, so a capacious closet is required. Either seek out an original or reproduction linen press, or have custom closets built, running the length of the landing, if possible, for maximum storage. Whichever is right for you, have the shelves set at levels appropriate for what they are to store. The lowest shelves are likely to be taller to stow quilts, comforters, and pillows, and higher ones closer together for quilt covers, sheets, and pillowcases.

Inspired solutions

◆ **Sort bedding by size** (twin, full, etc.) and function (top and fitted sheets, duvets, etc.) or simply keep whole sets together, and fold them neatly. Allocate a shelf or section of the shelf for each pile. As a folded single sheet looks much like a folded double, this will save you time in both choosing and putting them away.

◆ **Try to stack the pillowcases** by color to make for easier selection that will disturb the pile only once.

◆ **If there's space,** you could also store towels in the linen cupboard, relieving overburdened bathroom storage.

▶ **On the table**

Linens don't have to be stored in a closet. This painted console table kept on the landing has room underneath for a basket for pillows. The basket on top holds sheets and pillowcases.

▲ Shelf life

This pretty, white-painted cupboard lends charm to the landing, and it offers the ideal storage space with appropriately spaced shelves for blankets, quilts, and linens.

▲▲ Fresh color

The traditional linen cupboard often incorporated drawers as well as shelves. This one, which was originally left in the natural wood, has been painted in a traditional Swedish shade of gray to give it more contemporary appeal.

HALL TABLES & CONSOLES

The long, narrow space characteristic of many halls has traditionally led to the design of tall, slim hall and console tables with which to furnish them. Accessorized with a couple of table lamps, a vase of flowers, or paired with a hall mirror, they can turn a basic hall into a welcoming space. They are also useful for "parking" incoming mail, keys, and gloves. Most modern designs are elegant, narrow, and rectangular, while traditional console tables, especially from the Federal period, were half moon in shape, introducing a curved element to the hallway. These were often a table top with just two cabriole legs at the front, with the back supported by brackets. However, they could also be small semicircular chests, adding more hallway storage. You need not be limited to just console tables; any narrow piece of furniture can work well in the hall, so look for narrow chests of drawers, narrow cabinets, shelving units, and even narrow desks, which can have a double function, making excellent use of space.

Inspired solutions

◆ **Small surfaces soon fill up,** so try to keep hall tables clutter-free. Get in the habit of putting keys and loose change, for example, in the hall table drawer.

◆ **Invest in an attractive letter holder** to keep on the hall table so that mail can be kept firmly in line. If it has sections, mail can even be sorted for different family members as it is brought in.

◆ **A mirror hung above the console table** brings reflected light and focus to the area.

▶ **Mirror, mirror on the wall**
Mirrors are the perfect solution for doubling the visual effect of a room. This splendid narrow hall table takes the trick one step further by incorporating a mirror beneath it as well.

◀ Bureau of convenience

This slim white-painted secretary makes an excellent hall piece. Its pretty proportions and detailing provide a focal point, while the drawer, desk space, cubbyholes, and cupboard make for plenty of storage space.

▲ Classic beauty

This Federal-style, veneered, half-moon cabinet would give an elegant air to any period home and provide plenty of storage space behind the curved doors. Although it is situated in an open space here, its small dimensions would make it suitable in even a narrow hall.

◀ Bold statement

A chunky, stone-topped console makes a bold statement in the hallway, especially when teamed with just a few strong accessories.

SLIM SPACE SOLUTIONS

Whether you're planning the halls or landings, or under the stairway, the essential element common to all the connecting areas of the house is lack of space and the need for very shallow solutions. Although you'll be able to find furniture specially designed for hallways, there is no equivalent for landings.

The best answer for these upper levels is to make do with slender chests of drawers or cupboards, or have custom-designed, built-in closets. Hall furniture, by contrast, goes back centuries, and there is plenty available for every period of house. The beautiful curvy consoles of the Federal period offered the ultimate in elegant hall furniture and the Victorians developed new varieties of hat, coat, and umbrella stands. These endured throughout most of the twentieth century, joined by fresh new designs for cleaner, lighter hallways to greet the new millennium.

Timeless style

Classic hall trees, comprising hooks for coats, a top ledge for hats, and a bench for shoes and boots, make the ideal slim-line hall storage. They also offer a welcoming focal point. This buttermilk-painted version has a light, contemporary feel.

◄ **Space invaders**

The trick to creating the most storage is to make clever use of every square inch of space. This recess under the stairway has been fitted with display shelves, a creative use of what could have been wasted space.

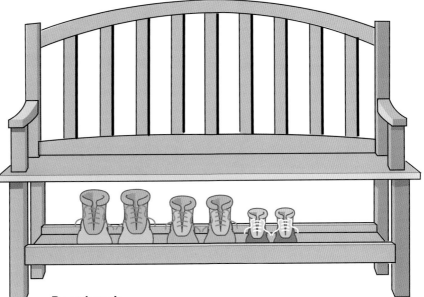

Boot bench

Here's the bench that thinks it's a boot store, combining good-looking hall furniture with a practical solution for storing shoes. The shelf under the bench stops any residual mud from falling onto the floor. This will prolong the life of the floor, as grit lodged in the soles of shoes has a sandpapering effect on hard surfaces.

Pegged out

This traditional Mission-style piece provides a useful combination of pegs for effective coat hanging plus mirrors, to introduce more light into the hallway.

Cool operator

The graceful lines of this Modern hat stand are a far cry from traditional Victorian curves, providing the perfect solution for contemporary homes.

Modern solution

Here's a console table that has essential storage for keys, gloves, and letters on the lower shelf, allowing you to leave the top free for just one elegant lamp or piece of sculpture.

WORK & PLAY

organized

efficient

neat

divided

shelves

closets

modern

hidden

files

boxed

bookstore

EFFICIENT SOLUTIONS

Where once a home office was seen as something of an extra, there are now few modern homes that do not allocate a room, or at least a substantial corner of a room, to office space. Ironically, although computers were expected to implement the paperless office, there are few of us who are ready for this. We still want to file all our utility bills, correspondence from banks, hospitals, doctors, lawyers, and accountants. We also need to store stationery, backup discs, and possibly audio discs. High-school students, too, need a workstation, either sharing the home office or in a corner of their own room. In addition to modern domestic office needs, the electronic revolution has enabled more and more of us to work from home, so there is a growing generation whose home office is also their workplace. All this adds up to the need for careful planning to ensure efficient storage with space for everything, while keeping everything under control so it doesn't threaten to infringe on the rest of your life and your home.

The starting point for office organization has to begin with the computer and all its peripherals. These have become less bulky with the introduction of flat screens and laptops, but you still need to allow space for the computer, printer, scanner, if you need one, and keyboard. You'll also need to think through organizing

▶▲ Compact workstation

A fabulously original workstation, which can be closed up at the end of the day behind the dark louvered doors is both practical and stylish.

▶ Open and shut case

With overhead cupboards and plenty of desktop drawers, there is ample storage space in this efficient home office. The desktop folding doors mean that when the job's done, it can simply be closed away.

◀ **Open-and-shut case**
Crafted out of closet space, there is plenty of storage space in this efficient home office. The folding doors close the office away when the job is done.

Bifold closet doors quickly shut away the paperwork, restoring bedroom peace and calm.

Shelves spanning the full width of the closet and set apart just an inch more than the tallest book make optimum use of the reference space.

A laptop is practical when open, even more so when closed, with no need for a separate processing unit— the perfect choice for a space-hungry office.

A separate drawer unit under the desk provides the perfect storage space for a simple lateral filing system, plus stationery and office supplies, such as staplers, hole punches, and calculators.

all the cabling (pending the day we become completely wireless). Many of the modern all-in-one workstations make this simple by providing space for each of these elements (see pages 152–153). However, Computer-Age Modern may not be your style, especially if the office is situated in part of another room. One solution could be to take a tip from traditional secretaries, where the office was essentially shut away into one piece of furniture. You may even be able to use a secretary to accommodate the computer and find another piece of furniture in keeping with the rest of your style to house the printer.

The computer problem solved, the next challenge is finding space for all the needed files, stationery, directories, discs, and books. For book storage, see pages 150–151. For everything else, the first decision is whether you would like to have everything on open shelves, behind closed doors, or a mixture of both.

With a wide range of attractive disc- and file-size boxes and containers available, it's becoming ever easier to keep shelves looking shipshape.

Whether you choose the concealed or the open-shelf route, aim to divide the space to fit the contents. So, for example, shelves designed to hold files should be one inch deeper than the file itself and set apart by the same height as the file, plus one inch. For stronger shelves, add vertical supports. If you have large files— legal files, for example—you may like to allow, say, six to each section, plus an extra inch for maneuverability. If you have open shelves, you could choose all-matching files for a cohesive look. This works well if you don't have too many, but over a certain number, say twelve, finding the right file can be time-consuming. Arrange them either alphabetically, or by number, or categorize the files themselves, choosing several different colors, one for each category.

▶ Twice the work

If computer space is all that is required, any shelf with space to pull up an office chair will do. Here, display shelves in this tiny sitting room double up as an office. The books, files, and general supplies are kept in a closet nearby.

▶▶ Drop top

This traditional secretary creates an excellent work surface as well as the perfect after work cover-up. With just two drawers under the desktop, the piece has a delightful open feel.

ALL-IN-ONE DESKS

Traditionally, home office work was carried out at a secretary with integral drawers and pigeon holes, often with a hinged top, which could simply be closed at the end of the job to cover up all reminders of tedious paperwork. Some of these desks consisted of a chest of drawers below the drop-down desktop plus cubbyholes above. These offer a reasonable amount of storage space for stationery, and even files that are compact enough to stow in drawers. However, those without the chest of drawers have minimal storage above the desk, suggesting these were more ladies' letter-writing desks than household workstations. They still make very decorative pieces, take up very little space, and can add charm to the living room, bedroom, or even the hall. For today's lifestyle, the older-style desk can be a great place for greeting cards and check writing and an inspiring place to work away from the main office, using a laptop.

Inspired solutions

◆ **If an elegant desk** suits your interior style but does not measure up in terms of storage space, position it near a closet—freestanding or built in—which can hold all the office needs.

◆ **Look for old desks and secretaries** in antique markets and junk shops. If they have a pretty shape, you can refurbish tired pieces by sanding the old finish and painting them with a soft, Swedish-inspired color, such as off-white, cream, gray-green, or gray-blue.

◆ **Use the individual drawers** to keep a handy supply of paper, envelopes, cards, and pens.

▶ **Contemporary style**
The clean lines of this modern-day desk incorporate a pullout desktop that would be excellent for use with a laptop. The printer could be stowed under the desk.

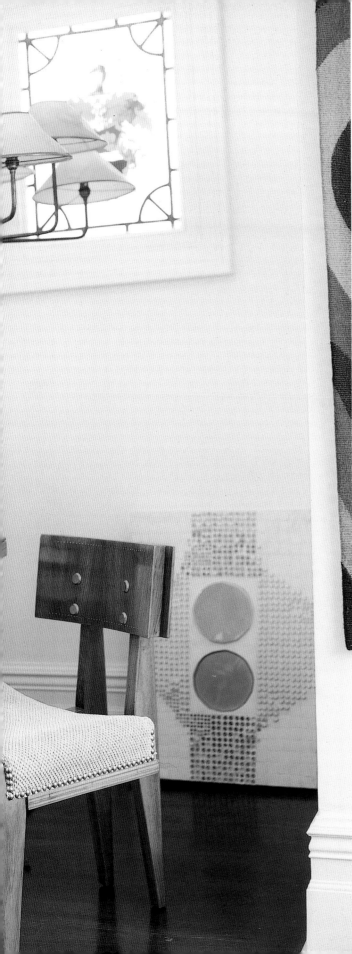

▲ Write at home

This elegant white-painted desk with slim, tapering legs would work well in the bedroom, suiting light social paperwork, such as writing greeting cards or checks.

KEEPING THE BOOKS

Books occupy a good percentage of most work areas, and the challenge is to provide enough space for them. So survey your work space and lay claim to every alcove, nook, and cranny—even the smallest can be used, if only for your tinier tomes. Think laterally when looking at the wall space. Is there any space around windows, for example; or above the door? When planning the shelving, you need to provide as much vertical support as possible. One way to do this is to divide the shelves vertically, and so limit the amount of weight that each section will be supporting.

Shelves can either be freestanding or built in. Your choice will depend on a combination of your own style and the architecture of the room. If you own a period home, built-in shelving will generally look more in keeping with traditional decorations, especially if you add baseboards and crown moldings to match the rest of the room. There's more flexibility in modern-style interiors (even in period houses), where both freestanding and built-in shelving looks good.

Inspired solutions

◆ **Allow for as many bookshelves** as you can. Even if you don't yet fill them up, it's likely you soon will, because book collections always seem to grow quickly and old books are so difficult to give away.

◆ **If you love the decorative look** of multicolored book spines, keep them on shelves. If not, put them in closets so they can be shut away out of sight.

▶ **Period style**
Bookshelves can be given a period feel by incorporating the correct architectural detailing. Here, the bookcases have been given crown molding and baseboards, and the cabinet doors are paneled. The muted green paint is also in keeping with the period styling of this room.

▶▶ **Up and over**
Custom-made bookshelves can be planned to use up every last square inch of space. These shelves occupy what would essentially be an unused wall, including over the top of the door, where useful but little-read books can be stored.

MODERN SOLUTIONS

The electronic age brings its own special demands to modern-day home office storage. The two main considerations are housing the hardware and finding a streamlined way to stow the stationery. Perhaps the simplest way to keep the hardware under control is to invest in one of the latest all-in-one workstations, which are designed to accommodate each of the various elements of a computer. The stationery is easiest to manage if it is subdivided within shelves using boxes, magazine holders, and stationery drawer inserts. If everything is behind closed doors, disparate files can line up on the shelves, but on open shelving, it's worth considering coordinated groups of boxes and containers for a more cohesive look. A third way is to choose a combination of open shelving and some closet space that can be shut away, which will have a more open look than closed cabinets, yet offer the option of concealing the messier elements.

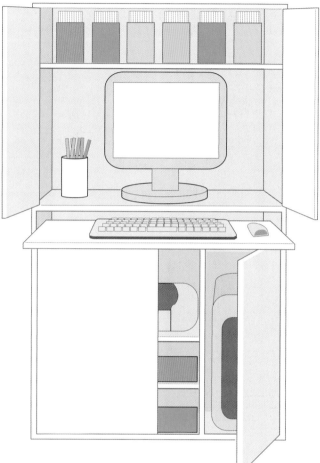

Home office hideaway

Store all you need for your home office in this chic white cupboard with sliding keyboard shelf. When the work is done, simply shut the doors and walk away.

◀ Adjustable space

Open shelving can look very attractive if carefully planned. This freestanding unit is designed to be a modular system, offering some taller and some shorter shelves to efficiently hold everything from DVDs to computer monitors.

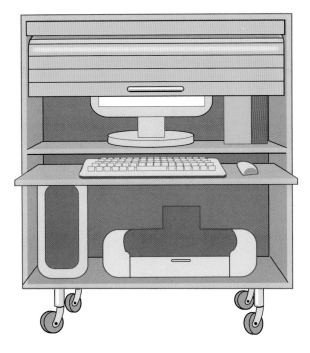

On a roll

Here's a simple solution—all you need accommodated in a smart modern cube. When the work day is over, simply pull down the roller panel to shut it all cleverly away. Mounted on lockable wheels, the whole unit is easily maneuverable. If you want it out of sight, just unplug the hardware and roll it away.

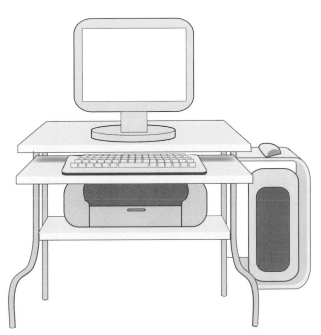

Down to basics

This workstation may be simple, but it nevertheless incorporates all the essential elements: a central processing unit (CPU) with a mouse pad on top, shelves for the monitor and keyboard, and a lower compartment to accommodate the printer.

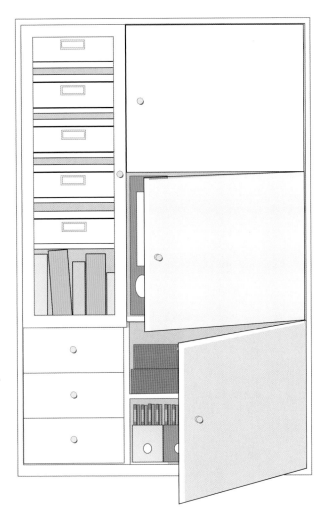

Stationery store

A combination of closed (or glass-front) cupboards and open shelving can be a useful solution for stationery. The open shelves create a more spacious feel than closed cupboards, but some stationery elements can veer toward the messy. Here, a coordinated group of boxes is used to store different-size envelopes, DVDs, and magazines. Files, the filing tray, and paper supply, which don't look so good, are kept behind doors, while drawer dividers make for efficient day-to-day stationery storage.

CHILDREN'S CRAFT & HOMEWORK AREAS

Even before children start school, they need a generous table for elementary art and craft work, though at this stage, this is more likely to be the kitchen table than anything else. However, once in school, they do like their own work space with a desk for reading and writing, plus storage space for books and stationery. As they grow older, this begins to take a more dominant role within the room, as children like to have their own space for working, and for storing and displaying souvenirs, projects, photographs, and records of school achievements. By the time they're in high school, they may even have their own workstation, complete with computer and peripherals. If you're short of space, one answer is to make a workstation under a loft bed in place of the lower bunk. However, this will work only if there's enough headroom in the space. Another solution is to buy an all-in-one desk that incorporates drawers for storage.

▼ Hide and seek

Locker-style drawers nesting under the bed add a fun element to a young girl's bedroom, and provide convenient and ample storage. A transparent wheeled container corrals handbags.

▲ Blue-ribbon storage

A large ribbon board hanging above a desk is a versatile graphic display and storage area for all those mementos. This room has been meticulously planned with open shelves on each side of the desk, perfect for any teenager.

▶▲ Sit on it

A windowseat that conceals storage is ideal in a bedroom, or any room. Here, it is complemented by a shelving unit whose height draws the eye up.

▶ A tisket, a tasket

This attractive set of baskets lends a significant design element while organizing sundry clothing, craft, and school items.

PERFECT PLANNING

The boundary between work and play is often blurred, but both are more satisfying if possessions are kept in check. Building blocks, jigsaws, and paper and pads need to be sorted into their own containers. Pens, pencils, paints, and paintbrushes need to be organized if they're going to be of any use. So plan for plenty of boxes of suitable sizes, then sort the contents into wide markers, fine-line pens, wax crayons, colored pencils, drawing pencils, and paintbrushes. Encourage the children to keep them in their boxes as they put everything away at bedtime, and then, every month or so, sort through them, throwing out any dried-up pens and stubby pencils. Also, provide plenty of bookshelves in work areas, preferably divided up to keep the books in better order.

Wheeled power

Plastic wheeled units, such as this one with custom-fit crates, make the perfect solution where space is tight. Every inch is used and the unit can easily be wheeled out of the way when not in use.

◀ Working developments

The under-bed space in this young child's room is used as a spare bed/sofa. However, as the child progresses to high school, the bed could be replaced with a metal-framed bed that incorporates a desk and bookshelves under the sleeping platform.

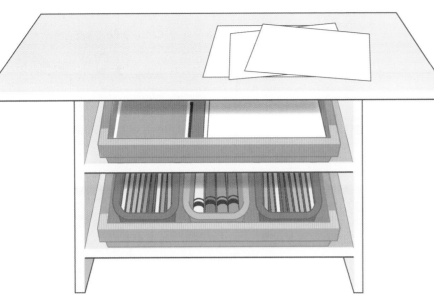

Combined effort

Look for children's furniture that combines storage with work surfaces. This table with space underneath for boxes containing paper, pads, pens, and pencils makes an ideal craft/work area.

On the go

Pretty wooden caddies are great for storing art needs, as they can be picked up and taken to another part of the house when needed. Inspired by tradesmen's equipment, their pretty colors make them appealing to children.

Easy access

These units are efficiently designed to hold storage boxes on dowel poles at a convenient angle so all the contents can be seen at a glance.

Team spirit

The combination of easy-reach bookshelves and plastic crate storage is ideal for work areas for children in elementary school.

PHOTOGRAPHY CREDITS

The publisher would like to thank the following photographers for supplying the pictures in this book:

Page 1 Carlos Domenech; **2** Antoine Bootz; **3** Jonn Coolidge; **4 top** Toshi Otsuki; **4 bottom** Edmund Barr; **5 top** Jonn Coolidge; **5 bottom** Carlos Domenech; **6** Luca Trovato; **8** Alexandre Bailhache; **9** Roger Davies; **10** Carlos Domenech; **11** Scott Frances; **12 left** Tim Beddow; **12 right** Fernando Bengoechea; **13** Gordon Beall; **14** Roger Davies; **15 top** Jacques Dirand; **15 bottom** Jeff McNamara; **17 top** Courtesy of *House Beautiful*; **17 bottom left** Luca Trovato; **17 bottom right** Guy Bouchet; **18** Jonn Coolidge; **19** Jacques Dirand; **21** Grey Crawford; **22 left** Jonn Coolidge; **22 right** Hugh Stewart; **23** Dana Gallagher; **24 top** Eric Roth; **24 bottom** Eric Roth; **25** Tim Beddow; **26 left** Simon Upton; **26 right** 1342 Studio; **27** Susan Gentry McWhinney; **28 top** Guy Bouchet; **28 bottom** Lizzie Himmel; **29** Fernando Bengoechea; **31** Oberto Gili; **32** Colleen Duffley; **33 top** Luke White; **33 bottom** Tria Giovan; **34** Michel Arnaud; **35** Jeff McNamara; **36** Dana Gallagher; **37 top** Jacques Dirand; **37 bottom** Jeff McNamara; **38** Pierre Chanteau; **39** William Waldron; **40 left** Gordon Beall; **40 right** Oberto Gili; **41** William Waldron; **42 top** Erik Kvalsvik; **42 bottom** William Waldron; **43 top left** David Montgomery; **43 top right** Guy Bouchet; **43 bottom left** Elizabeth Zeschin; **43 bottom right** Dominique Vorillon; **44** Tim Street-Porter; **44 top** Antoine Bootz; **44 bottom** Carlos Emilio; **47** Gridley & Graves; **48 left** Oberto Gili; **48 right** Tim Street-Porter; **49** Peter Woloszynski; **50 top** Peter Margonelli; **50 bottom** Colleen Duffley; **51** Tria Giovan; **52** Toshi Otsuki; **53 top** Toshi Otsuki; **53 bottom** Toshi Otsuki; **54** Thibault Jeanson; **55 top** Laura Resen; **55 bottom** Michael James O'Brien; **56** Dominique Vorillon; **57** Guy Bouchet; **58** Richard Bryant/Arcaid; **59** Jacques Dirand; **60** Eric Piasecki; **61 top** Valerio Mezanotti; **61 bottom** Fernando Bengoechea; **62** Pieter Estersohn; **63** Carolyn Englefield; **64 top** Tria Giovan; **64 bottom** Laura Resen; **65 top** Peter Estersohn; **65 bottom** Jacques Dirand; **66 left** Tim Street-Porter; **66 right** Christopher Drake; **67** Jeff McNamara; **68** Tria Giovan; **69** Peter Margonelli; **70** 1342 Studio; **71 top** Maura McEvoy; **71 bottom** Scott Frances; **72 left** Gordon Beall; **72 right** Scott Frances; **73 right** Alec Hemer; **74 top** Guy Bouchet; **74 bottom** Guy Bouchet; **75 left** Grey Crawford; **75 top right** Bruce Buck; **75 bottom right** Oberto Gili; **76 left** Fernando Bengoechea; **76 right** Jonn Coolidge; **77 top** Francois Dischinger; **77 bottom** John M. Hall; **78** Jonn Coolidge; **79** Victoria Pearson; **80** Toshi Otsuki; **81** Jonn Coolidge; **82** Jonn Coolidge; **83** Gordon Beall; **84** Eric Roth; **85** Dominique Vorillon; **86** David Montgomery; **87 top** Tim Street-Porter; **87 bottom** Oberto Gili; **88 left** Courtesy of *House Beautiful*; **88 right** Jeff McNamara; **89 top right** Edmund Barr; **89 bottom right** Carlos Domenech; **90 top** Christophe Dugied; **90 bottom** Tim Street-Porter; **91** Fernando Bengoechea; **92** Guy Bouchet; **93** Victoria Pearson; **94** Jonn Coolidge; **95** Fernando Bengoechea; **96** Curtis Taylor; **97 top** Guy Bouchet; **97 bottom** Oberto Gili; **98** Tom McWilliam; **99** Jeff McNamara; **100** Antoine Bootz; **101** Susie Cushner; **102** Christophe Dugied; **103 top** Scott Frances; **103 bottom** Gloria Nichol; **104 left** Jonn Coolidge; **104 top right** Pieter Estersohn; **104 bottom right** Luca Trovato; **105 top left** Simon Upton; **105 top right** Steve Freihon; **105 bottom** Dana Gallagher; **106** Elizabeth Zeschin; **107 top** Oberto Gili; **107 bottom** Eric Boman; **108 left** Tom McWilliam; **108 right** Christopher Drake; **109** Jonn Coolidge; **110** Simon McBride; **111** Tria Giovan; **112 left** Melanie Acevedo; **112 right** Jonn Coolidge; **113** Minh + Wass; **114** Staffan Johansson; **115** Simon Upton; **116** Erik Kvalsvik; **117 top** Thibault Jeanson; **117 bottom** Roger Davies; **118 left** Jonn Coolidge; **118 right** René Stoeltie; **119** Colleen Duffley; **120 top** Christopher Drake; **120 bottom** Chirstopher Drake; **121** Jonn Coolidge; **122 top** Jonn Coolidge; **122 bottom** Roger Davies; **123** Barbara and René Stoeltie; **124** Jeff McNamara; **125 top** Erica Lennard; **125 bottom** Tim Street-Porter; **126** Alexandre Bailhache; **127 top** William Waldron; **127 bottom** Eric Roth; **128** Richard Felber; **129** Tim Street-Porter; **130** Eric Piasecki; **131 top** Jonn Coolidge; **131 bottom** William Waldron; **132** William Waldron; **133 left** Fernando Bengoechea; **133 top** Tom Crane; **133 bottom** Jeff McNamara; **134 top** Pieter Estersohn; **134 bottom** Fernando Bengoechea; **135** Polly Eltes; **136 left** Jeff McNamara; **136 right** Alec Hemer; **137** Peter Estersohn; **138** William Waldron; **139** William Waldron; **140** Jeff McNamara; **141** Jonn Coolidge; **142** François Dischinger; **143** Jeremy Samuleson; **144** Roger Davies; **145** Tom McWilliam; **146 bottom** Fernando Bengoechea; **146 top** Gordon Beall; **147** Ted Loos; **148 left** Gordon Beall; **148 right** Eric Piasecki; **149 top** William Waldron; **149 bottom** Susan Gilmore; **150** Fritz von der Schulenburg; **151** Tom McWilliam; **152 left** Simon Upton; **152 right** Polly Eltes; **153** Scott Frances; **154** Oberto Gili; **155** Thibault Jeanson; **156 left** Victoria Pearson; **156 right** Matthew Milman; **157 top** Peter Aaron/Esto; **157 bottom** Fernando Bengoechea.

INDEX